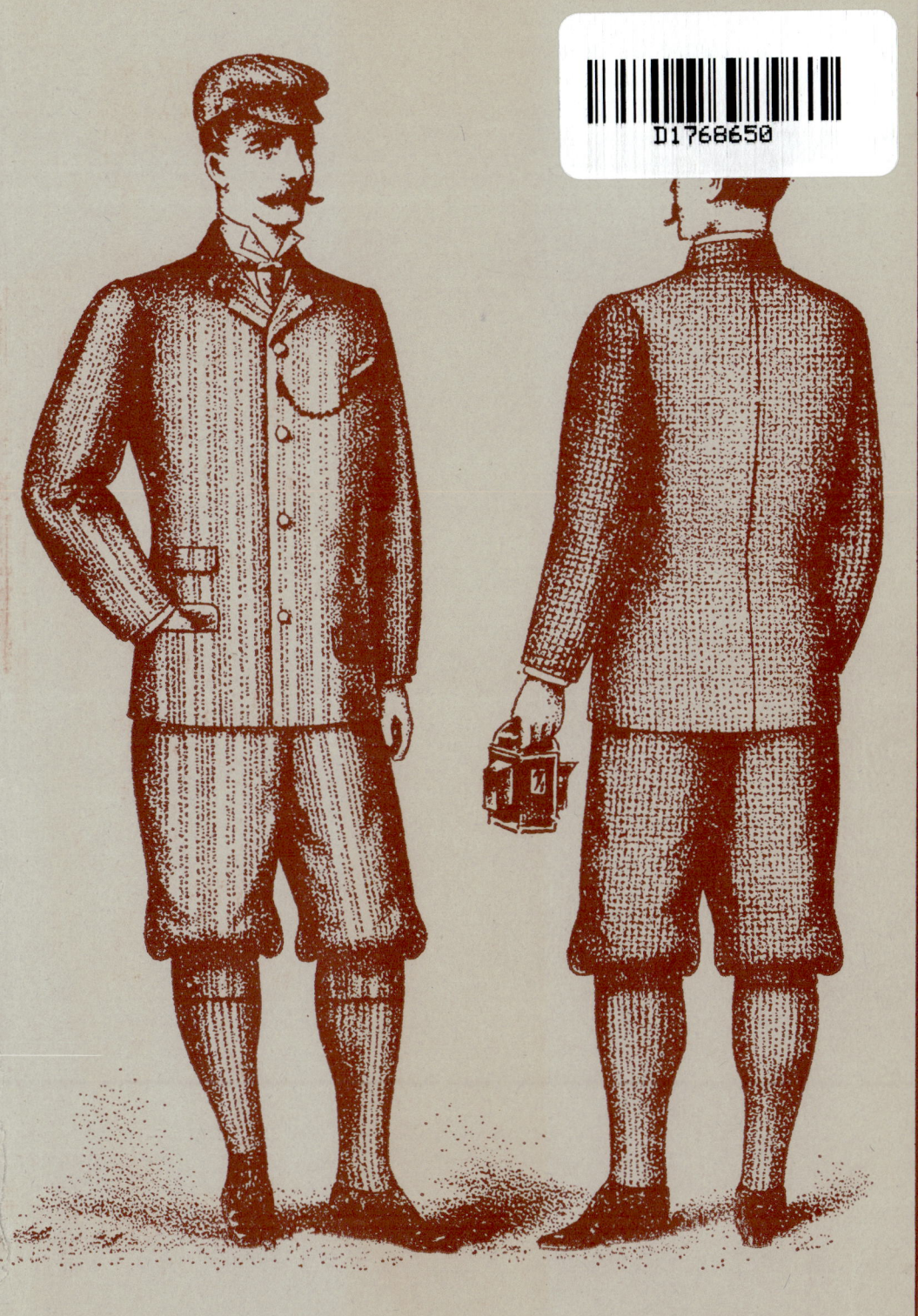

The Saturday Book

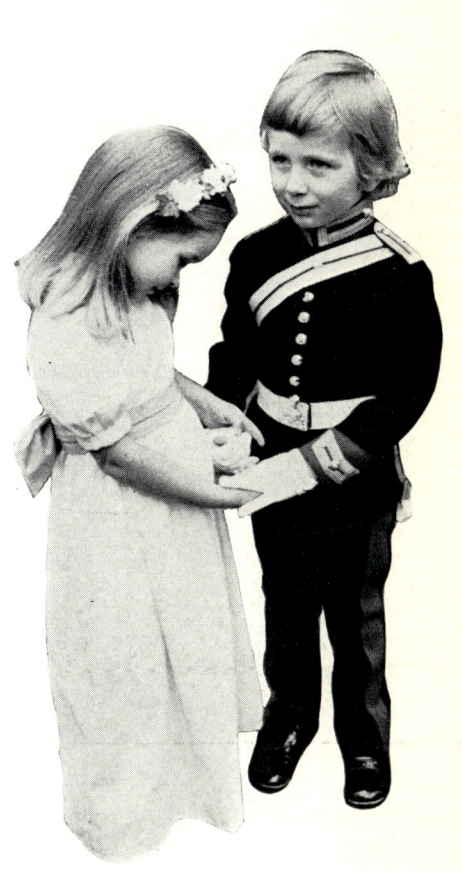

CHARDIN: *La gouvernante*, 1738 (National Gallery of Canada, Ottawa)

The Saturday Book

EDITED BY JOHN HADFIELD

29

HUTCHINSON OF LONDON

THE SATURDAY BOOK was founded in 1941 by Leonard Russell and has been edited since 1952 by John Hadfield. This twenty-ninth annual issue has been made and printed in Great Britain by The Anchor Press Ltd and bound by William Brendon & Son Ltd, both of Tiptree, Essex.

© Hutchinson & Company (Publishers) Ltd 1969

09 099280 6

Introduction

CRITICS, according to that Jacobean man of letters Sir Henry Wotton, are merely 'brushers of noblemen's clothes'. But after reading the critics' notices of the last issue of THE SATURDAY BOOK we found ourselves feeling in our pockets for tenpenny pieces, or even half-dollars, to press upon these literary cloakroom attendants. Far from giving THE SATURDAY BOOK the conventional brush-off, they had written in the most flattering terms about its cut, its cloth, its style. 'The youngest-looking grown-up annual of the lot' was one comment. 'The most enterprising of the seasonal annuals' was another. No less an arbiter of pop fashion than *The Times* wrote: 'It gives the young trendies something to imitate'.

The emphasis on the youthful figure and the air of enterprise was especially gratifying to the editor of an annual that has been frequenting the bookstores and tottering from the bar of El Vino to the armchairs of the Algonquin for no less than twenty-eight successive years. Then a sobering thought struck us. Maybe the critics (for once) were being sentimental, kind; and were just giving us the Ginger Rogers treatment.

Perish the ageing thought! We recognise—and proudly recognise—that very few annuals apart from *Whitaker's Almanack*, *Who's Who*, and the Sears Roebuck Catalogue have run uninterruptedly for as long a period as our own, but we draw your attention to the fact that we are still—just—in our twenties. 'The roaring twenties' is a term that comes to mind. In our twenty-ninth number we propose to continue our cultivation of the nurseries of blooming youth, before we pass into our geriatric thirties. Perhaps it is a sign of virility—or at least a symptom of the seven-year itch—that we have just changed our American publisher as light-heartedly as a young man-about-town changes his mistress.

So, yet again, the opening chorus is the Young Idea. After some hymns to Hymen, the god of marriage, who was believed to be the son of Apollo, we put on a show of the male counterparts of the dolls, birds or girl friends who were the opening feature of last year's issue—in other words, the god Apollo him-

Introduction

self, in the various shapes and guises in which he has manifested himself through the ages, from the young pharaoh Akhnaton down to Mick Jagger. Thence it is a natural progression to studies of the Art of Seduction, the Arts of Attraction, and—a slice of real Saturdiurnalia—Great Lovers of the Silent Screen.

It is our editorial view, however (whether or not the Doctors Kronhausen would agree), that eighty-five out of two hundred and fifty-six pages is an adequate allowance for sex—at the age of twenty-nine. The rest of the book, therefore, is the usual mish-mash of art and travel, running the gamut from Hammond Innes on cave-paintings to J. B. Priestley on 'holiday painting', from topiary to toy theatres, from the art of conducting (by Malcolm Sargent's biographer) to a vision of Romantic America through the eyes of a brilliant New Zealand painter, from the throwing of pots to the putting together of jigsaw puzzles.

This last topic is perhaps peculiarly relevant to THE SATURDAY BOOK (apart from the fact that collecting old jigsaws is probably the 'trend' we are initiating this year, just as in past years we pioneered the vogue for beards, *Art Nouveau*, old traction engines and the works of Aubrey Beardsley). A few lines back we used the word 'mish-mash', which has delighted us ever since it was applied to our production by that doyen of book-producers, Sir Francis Meynell. 'Mish-mash' is a good description of our contents. But the actual assembly of our material, and its composition into some sort of disorderly shape, calls for much the same ingenuity, patience and cranky enjoyment as does the putting together of a jigsaw puzzle. We only hope that the result is as gay and colourful, if not necessarily as self-improving, as the splendid examples in Mrs Hannas's collection.

J.H.

The endpaper design reproduces 'Gamage's Newest Styles in Cycling Suits', from Gamage's first Christmas Catalogue, 1893. The photograph on page 1, preceding the frontispiece, is of Peter Cobbold, aged four, and Emma Peto, aged three, who were attendants at a wedding in the Guards Chapel in January 1969.

Contents

A LOOKING GLASS FOR LOVERS

Hymns to Hymen: Ancient and Modern	9
Madge Garland: The Male Image	18
James Laver: The Art of Seduction	53
Raymond Lamont Brown: Arts of Attraction	65
Rodney Ackland: Love without Words	76

PICTURESQUE TOURS

Georgina Mase: Autumn Night on the Dordogne	95
Hammond Innes: The Country of the Caves	96
Miles Hadfield: On Fountains Drawings by Michael Felmingham	108
Felix Kelly: Romantic America Commentary by Robert Harling	126

A MISH-MASH OF THE ARTS

Fred Bason: A Date with a Dame	139
J. B. Priestley: A Holiday Painter	145
Charles Reid: A Gallery of Conductors Photographs by Erich Auerbach	157
James Blades: The Man behind the Drums	177
Olive Cook: The Curious Art of Topiary Photographs by Edwin Smith	192
George Speaight: The Brigand in the Toy Theatre	205
Linda Hannas: Joys of the Jigsaw	216
Tony Birks: Making a Pot	233
David Cheshire: Male Impersonators	245

A LOOKING GLASS FOR LOVERS

Hymns to Hymen
ANCIENT AND MODERN

THE ENJOYMENT

CLASPED in the arms of her I love,
  In vain, alas! for life I strove;
  My fluttering spirits, wrapped in fire
  By love's mysterious art,
Borne on the wings of fierce desire,
  Flew from my flaming heart.

Thus lying in a trance for dead,
Her swelling breasts bore up my head,
When, waking from a pleasing dream,
  I saw her killing eyes,
Which did in fiery glances seem
  To say: 'Now Celia dies.'

Fainting, she pressed me in her arms,
And trembling lay, dissolved in charms,
When, with a shivering voice, she cried:
  'Must I alone then die?'
'No, no,' I languishing replied,
  'I'll bear thee company . . .'

THOMAS OTWAY
Published 1709, written c. 1680

HEAVEN OF BEAUTY

THIS HOUR be her sweet body all my song,
   Now the same heart-beat blends her gaze with mine,
   One parted fire, Love's silent countersign:
Her arms lie open, throbbing with their throng
Of confluent pulses, bare and fair and strong:
   And her deep-freighted lips expect me now,
   Amid the clustering hair that shrines her brow
Five kisses broad, her neck ten kisses long.

Lo, Love! thy heaven of Beauty; where a sun
   Thou shin'st; and art a white-winged moon to press
   By hidden paths to every hushed recess;
Yea, and with sinuous lightnings here anon
Of passionate change, an instant seen and gone,
   Shalt light the tumult of this loveliness.

            DANTE GABRIEL ROSSETTI, 1869

A THING OF BEAUTY

AS BLUE is golden
   In the pools of springtime
   As green is amber
In your waking eyes
As tongues are songless
In the deeps of loving
So air is wingless
When the last bird flies;

Though words are wingless
And the eyes know blindness
Though hands are powerless
To hold at bay
The tears of autumn
And the ache of winter
No grief this present
Shall steal away;

For your breasts are mallows
In the fields of summer
Your breath is promise
On the winds of chance
Your hair is willows
In the drift of rivers
Where your heart lies calm
In love's sensuous trance;

Your hands stray over
My limbs in loving
Not even the sun
Brings such sweet light
A thing of beauty
In my arms at noontide
Whose radiance mellows
The oblivious night;

As blue is amber
In the groves of autumn
And green is golden
In your sleeping eyes
Love is the essence
Of the old world's breathing
And Now is the air
Through which the first bird flies.

JOHN SMITH, 1969

Hymns to Hymen

GIRL UNDER FIG-TREE

SLIM GIRL, slow burning
   quick to run
   under the fig-tree's
loaded fruits.

Skin-cold like them
your wet teeth spread,
parting pink
effervescent lips.

When I hold you here
valleys of fruit and flesh
bind me
now wet, now dry.

While on your eyes, the cool
green-shaded lids
close on the
wells of summer.

Slim girl, slow burning
quick to rise
between question
and loaded promise.

If I take you, peel you
against the noonday dark,
blind wasps
drill my hands like stars.

LAURIE LEE, 1969

GIRL ON BANK OF PINKS AND LILIES

Do not ask me, charming Phillis,
   Why I lead you here alone,
By this bank of pinks and lilies
   And of roses newly blown.

'Tis not to behold the beauty
   Of those flowers that crown the spring;
'Tis to—but I know my duty,
   And dare never name the thing.

('Tis, at worst, but her denying;
   Why should I thus fearful be?
Every minute, gently flying,
   Smiles and says, 'Make use of me.')

What the sun does to those roses,
   While the beams play sweetly in,
I would—but my fear opposes,
   And I dare not name the thing.

Yet I die, if I conceal it;
   Ask my eyes, or ask your own;
And if neither can reveal it,
   Think what lovers think alone.

On this bank of pinks and lilies,
   Might I speak what I would do;
I would wish my lovely Phillis—
   I would; I would—Ah! would *you*?

                ANONYMOUS
                in *The Hive*, 1724

TRUE BLUE

Woke up this morning
in the middle of winter
salt in my coffee
sweat in my hair,
the letter said SHE'S DEAD,
WE KNOW YOU WILL MISS HER
woke up this morning
in winter in winter.

Started to answer
but couldn't remember
the clothes that she wore
or the things that we said.
Wrote I was sorry
would be there on Thursday;
found myself busy
sent flowers instead.

Several girls later
I met her while dreaming;
sullen, untidy,
her hands in her hair,
lovely as ever,
I'VE GOT TO GET STARTED
she shouted, GET STARTED,
and parted the air.

Woke up this morning
in the middle of winter
salt in my coffee
sweat in my hair,
I could remember
us sleeping together
and how she wore nothing
in winter in winter.

CHRISTOPHER LOGUE, 1969

SEVENTEENTH-CENTURY BLUES

No, no, poor suffering heart, no change endeavour;
Choose to sustain the smart, rather than leave her.
My ravished eyes behold such charms about her,
I can die with her, but not live without her:
One tender sigh of hers, to see me languish,
Will more than pay the price of my past anguish:
Beware, oh cruel fair, how you smile on me!
'Twas a kind look of yours that has undone me.

Love has in store for me one happy minute,
And she will end my pain who did begin it;
Then no day void of bliss or pleasure leaving,
Ages shall slide away without perceiving:
Cupid shall guard the door, the more to please us,
And keep out Time and Death, when they would seize us:
Time and Death shall depart, and say, in flying,
'Love has found out a way to live by dying.'

JOHN DRYDEN, 1692

Hymns to Hymen

POEM ON FEBRUARY THE FOURTEENTH

to my wife

Dear, now that the cold is on the crocus
I should feel the ache of something missing:
snows mush and melt and small lights fall
from twigs—such high notes beyond hearing;
indoors, the piano plays the sound of felt.

Only our intemperate youth has been pilfered,
not our tenderness—neither yours nor mine.
For love is no less because less uttered
or more accepted. You, you, still my valentine!
And what has been added is not missing.

Just one note gone. The rest all candid sound,
and outside, night skies, too, seem no emptier
after a shooting star—so with us.
Footprints in the snow vanish with the snow,
but my love is because of what you are.

DANNIE ABSE, 1969

POEM IN MIDDLE AGE

THE FIRE of love in youthful blood,
   Like what is kindled in brushwood,
     But for a moment burns;
Yet in that moment makes a mighty noise,
It crackles, and to vapour turns,
   And soon itself destroys.

But when crept into agëd veins
It slowly burns, and long remains;
   And, with a sullen heat,
Like fire in logs, it glows, and warms 'em long,
And, though the flame be not so great,
   Yet is the heat as strong.

               CHARLES SACKVILLE
               EARL OF DORSET
               1690

The Male Image

BY MADGE GARLAND

THE IDEAL of male beauty has varied far less than that of its female counterpart. At various periods and places women with large buttocks, pregnant bellies, huge bosoms, or none at all, have been admired; but from the earliest-known rock-paintings to the present day the hunter, the god, the hero and the lover have all been presented as broad-shouldered, small-waisted and slender-hipped. To this basic standard certain cultures have added special characteristics: the straight profile of a Greek statue, the broad brow and stern chin of a Roman emperor, the wide-apart blue eyes of the Northerner, or the dark oval face of the Southerner; but the most widely acknowledged example of male good looks is the sculpture of classical Greece; to be likened to a Greek god has been the ultimate compliment for over two thousand years.

Is it still? To a generation for whom Ringo Starr is billed as the new screen lover the classic profile might well no longer appeal. Modern taste would be more likely to agree with Francis Bacon when he said 'there is no exquisite beauty without some strangeness in the proportion'. But this strangeness was limited to the physiognomy. The figure remains the same as that admired thousands of years ago: the narrow hips of the Minoan cup-bearer, the slender legs of quattrocento pages, are still required by the universal blue jeans of today.

Even pop-singers, who bear no resemblance to the *ephebes* of the ancient world or to the youthful beauty admired in the Middle Ages, conform with regard to their nether-limbs. When the panache of the courtier gave way to the understatement of the gentleman, taste did not change; although at some periods a small waist was required it was always essential, whether in short tunics, court breeches or long trousers, for legs to be long and hips slender.

Only the profile has wavered. Since the last war individuality has become more important than regular features. The variety of the baroque has triumphed over classic regularity.

William Poyntz, aged 18. Painted in 1762 by Thomas Gainsborough (Coll. Earl Spencer, Althorp)

IN ANTIQUITY

The vase painting opposite, on an Attic amphora in the British Museum, *circa* 430 B.C., shows a contemporary cartoon of a well-known scandal, an archaic Apollo being embraced by an enthusiastic Helen, whose hair is seized by her understandably exasperated husband Menelaus.

The recent discoveries of Etruscan art have thrown a new light on the Apollo on the right, with his enigmatic smile. His profile follows the classical formula of forehead and nose in one unbroken line; his hair, bound with a fillet, is carefully combed, with curls over the forehead and long twists falling on his shoulders. (Apollo da Vejo, now in the Museo di Villa Giulia, Rome. Photo: Mansell)

One of the earliest and rarely surpassed examples of the masculine superlative is the pharaoh Akhnaton (left), with his narrow head and upward-slanting eyes, a type unknown in northern Europe. Elongated headforms have been admired by different races all over the world, though some, like the Chinook Indians, have preferred a flattened forehead. Drastic artificial methods have been used to alter the natural shape of the skull and mothers have gone to the extreme of compressing the skulls of their infants between wooden boards in order that their children should be in the fashion. The practice of binding children's heads continued in France until the nineteenth century, and was still practised in Africa in the twentieth. (Vatican Museum: photo, Mansell Collection)

THE CLASSICAL IDEAL

Two examples of plastic male beauty which are universally accepted as representing the ideal are the Belvedere Apollo (left; Vatican Museum: photograph, Mansell Collection) and Antinous (right). To these classical figures modern youth approximates only in physical development, luxuriance of coiffure, and a return to nudity, or near-nudity, as a normal condition. The Belvedere Apollo's more muscular torso and strong legs are more to contemporary taste than Antinous' rather too fleshy body, but Professor G. M. A. Hanfmann says of this marble statue of a one-time slave: 'In his life the boy from Asia Minor was worshipped by Hadrian, after death by the entire Roman world. His sultry features are here idealised after a late classical model.' The beauty of the feet of both figures is particularly striking to a generation accustomed to uncared-for extremities, ruined by footwear. Apollo's sandals might well be revived by a shoe-designer today, though the feet which would wear them might not resemble the originals. The god's coiffure might be considered too *recherchée* even for Chelsea, but Antinous' mop of curls, perhaps less carefully arranged, is constantly to be seen in the King's Road. The Antinous statue comes from Hadrian's villa at Tivoli, and is now in the Museo Nazionale, Naples.

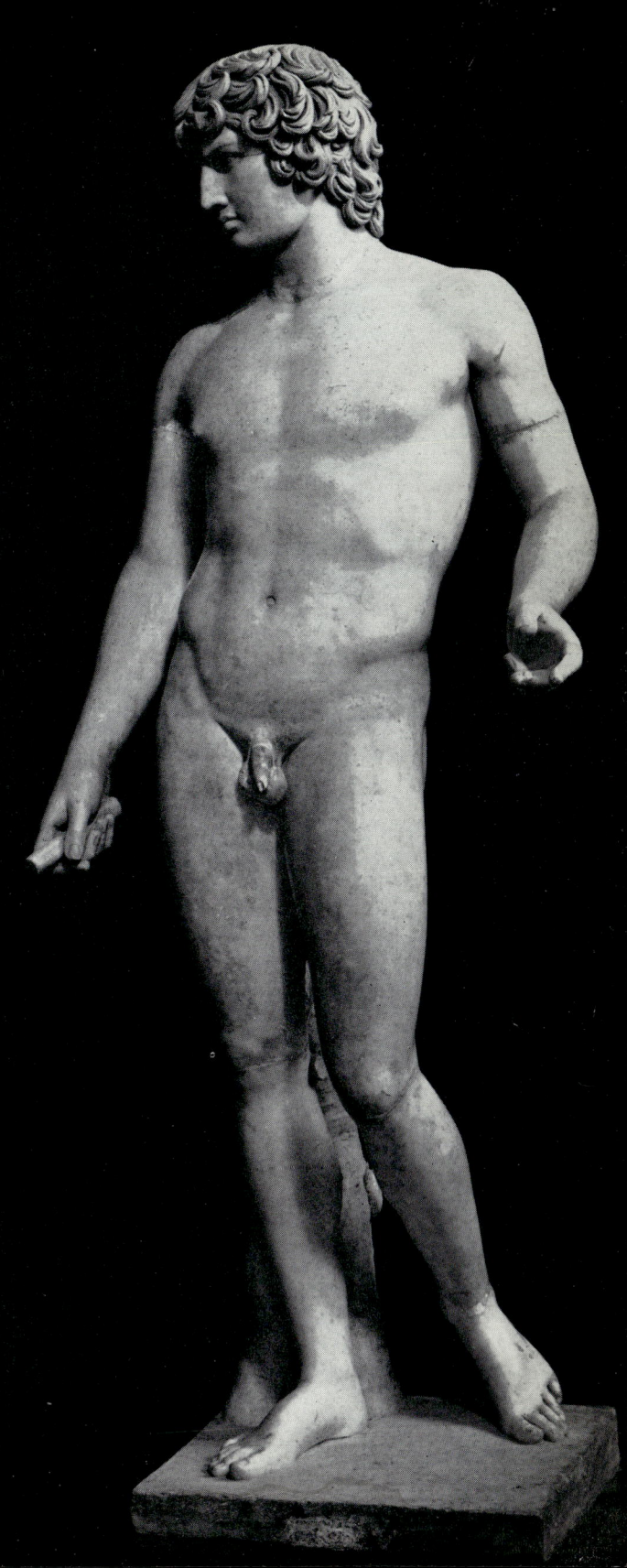

RENAISSANCE MAN

The Renaissance revived the classical ideal of the male body perfect in proportions and details, but to it added a warmth and feeling for individual character often lacking in antique works of art. Michelangelo's 'David' (opposite; Galleria dell Accademia, Florence: photo, Mansell Collection) illustrated this fusion of the rules of Pericles with the new spirit of the quattrocento, whose perfect man was not only of great physical beauty but keenly aware of the vast new possibilities opened to him both by a rediscovery of ancient cultures and the new discoveries in learning. Portraits began to emphasise the varied personalities of the sitters and to give examples of the different types then admired. Palma Vecchio's noble 'Poet' (above, on the right), has shoulder-length hair brushed back from the forehead, a slight beard and moustache, and the dreamy expression associated with his craft. His low-cut jerkin reveals a white pleated chemisette and large and elaborate sleeves; several necklaces of small chains hang round his bare neck. The alert expression and capable hands of Andrea del Sarto's clean-shaven 'Young Sculptor' (below), and his simple and workmanlike attire, are singularly different from that of the thoughtful poet. (Both pictures on this page from the National Gallery, London)

In the Giovanni Bellini portrait above of a young man and his tutor (private collection, England) the latter looks somewhat quizzically at the boy's extravagant coiffure, known as a *zazzera*, in which the long hair was pomaded and stiffened until it stood away from the head in a most curious shape. The youth painted by Sandro Botticelli (opposite) wears his hair dressed simply with a centre parting and with locks which reach his high collar, framing his long, sensitive face. (Collection, Sir Thomas Merton.) The young man on the left, painted by Jacometto Veneziano (National Gallery) wears a more conventional Renaissance coiffure, variations of which are often seen today. 20

HAIR DRESSING

Men's hair today is once again an important attribute, though only twenty years ago it was of negligible account, and it almost vanished in the 'fifties, when the 'crew-cut' brought near-baldness into fashion. Albrecht Dürer (above; Prado, Madrid) painted himself in 1498 at the age of twenty-seven with his curly hair more than shoulder-length, which, together with moustache and beard, gives him a remarkably modern air. Equally up-to-date in a different style is that of Philip Otto Runge's self-portrait, dated 1802, on the page opposite (Kunsthalle, Hamburg).

The sixteenth century saw the most extraordinary opulence in men's costume, and the court of Henri III of France particularly was famous for its extravagance. The *mignons* above, beloved by the King, described by a contemporary as 'unpleasantly unnatural to look at', vied with each other in the splendour of their attire. Three of them were painted together in similar striped silk costumes and tiny ruffs, each wearing different ear-rings, and with their curled hair brushed back from their clean-shaven faces and decorated in a variety of ways with ribbons, bows and jewels. (Anonymous; private collection; photo, Colnaghi)

FACE DRESSING

François I's beauty, legendary in his own day, is difficult to deduce from his many portraits: the eyes too small, the nose too long for current taste; but the eyebrows are finely drawn and the cleft chin is not concealed by his small beard. François' hair was cut short after an accident, so setting a fashion soon followed by his neighbour-king, Henry of England. The painting on the left is attributed to Clouet (Louvre, Paris). The pointed shape of King Charles' beard (right) became known as a Van Dyck after the artist who so fortuitously recorded in three poses the sensitive face of the doomed king. (Reproduced by gracious permission of H.M. the Queen.)

The ultimate in beards is undoubtedly that of the famous Fath Ali Shah of Persia (right) who transmitted this characteristic to his sons, many of whom also were painted with long black beards. (Royal Library, Windsor, reproduced by gracious permission of H.M. the Queen.) The miniaturist Nicholas Hilliard (right centre) painted his own portrait, aged thirty in 1577, wearing a rakish short beard (Victoria and Albert Museum, London.) When Richard Burton (far right) went to Oxford in 1840 he thought the clean-shaven undergraduates looked like children. The authorities forced him to cut off his moustaches but he made good this deprivation in later life, and when Louis Desanges painted him in 1861 he exhibited shoulder-length face ornaments.

HEAD DRESSING

A high-crowned hat has been a symbol of high life for hundreds of years, and seventeenth-century Dutch burghers, when out courting, wore tall chimney-pot hats like those shown in 'Country Courtships' by Willem Buytewich (Rijksmuseum, Amsterdam). The 'topper' did not take on its present form until the latter part of the nineteenth century, when it was worn by gentlemen and workmen alike, and in the country as well as at formal gatherings. Black was for everyday wear but grey for special occasions, and Somerset Maugham (left) was painted in a pale grey 'topper', ready for Ascot in 1911, by Gerald Kelly (Photo, Royal Academy).

The portrait of the youth who became known as the 'handsomest young man in England' was painted by Frau Ewald when Rupert Brooke was staying with her in Germany in 1912. This modern Apollo was described by David Garnett as 'tall and well-built'; and he added: 'his complexion, his skin, his eyes and hair were perfect'. (Reproduced by courtesy of the Provost and Fellows, King's College, Cambridge.) William Augustus Bowles (left) was an adventurer who fought with the British forces in America, and visited England in the 1790s with a party of Indian chiefs, when Thomas Hardy painted him wearing a head-dress similar to those of his Indian friends. (Bearsted Collection, Upton House, reproduced by permission of the National Trust)

THE ROMANTIC IMAGE

The young men of the romantic era wore their own hair long and wind-blown, but were clean-shaven. During the 1830's there were said to be only two beards in the whole of Paris: that of Achille Déveria, one of the two gifted artist-brothers, and that of Petrus Borel, known as the Lycanthrope or man-wolf, whose beard was thought to give him a resemblance to a portrait by El Greco.

The pre-Raphaelites paid particular attention to hair, and when Dante Gabriel Rossetti painted his own portrait (above, National Portrait Gallery) in the mid-century his hair was long, slightly curled and rather untidy. The artist's questioning eyes and sensuous nose and mouth are in strong contrast to the features of the young Franz Liszt (left) whose soft straight hair frames an exceptionally sensitive face but which gives the owner an air of knowing exactly what he could and would achieve. (Drawing of Liszt by Achille Déveria, 1832; private collection; photo, Hartnell & Aird)

MORE ROMANTIC IMAGES

The ethereal quality which made Shelley so beloved of women is charmingly expressed in this posthumous portrait by Joseph Severn, Keats' friend, painted in 1845 against a landscape of the picturesque ruins so much admired by both poets (Keats-Shelley Memorial House, Rome). An air of brooding, of pastoral peace, pervades the whole composition, which shows the young poet with pen in his hand, ready to write.

In emulation of the Elizabethan recumbent portraits which he greatly admired, such as that of Lord Herbert by Isaac Oliver in which the subject, still holding his shield and clad in splendid blue satin and lace, lies full length on the ground, Sir Brooke Boothby (opposite) was painted by Joseph Wright of Derby (Tate Gallery) in brown knee-breeches and light hose reclining against a tree stump. The setting of a woodland glade was particularly suited to one who was a friend of Jean-Jacques Rousseau, some of whose work Sir Brooke helped to publish. Such rural backgrounds and informal poses were less unusual when Rex Whistler, also wearing breeches and light hose, but minus the elegance of Sir Brooke's large tie and splendid hat, lay down beneath a tree to play his guitar for Cecil Beaton, not long before the last war, in which Whistler was killed. These visions of dreaming men, poet, philosopher or artist in tranquil surroundings, with time for meditation, illustrate a way of life fast vanishing, if not already gone, from our midst.

ENGLISH ELEGANCE

Few Englishmen ever surpassed in beauty of person and costume the unknown love-sick courtier (above) who, leaning against a rose-encircled tree, proclaimed 'My praisëd faith procures my pain'. The miniature is by Nicholas Hilliard, c. 1590 (Victoria and Albert Museum). Nearly two hundred years later William Beckford (left), rich, elegant and imaginative, famous for the building of Fonthill Abbey and the translation of the Arabian tale of *Vathek*, both in their respective ways equally strange and gloomy, posed against a classical pediment for George Romney. (Bearsted Collection, Upton House, reproduced by permission of the National Trust)

FRENCH ELEGANCE

French elegance is of a very different breed from the English, less picturesque, more carefully contrived. Even Ingres' portrait of the handsome François-Marius Granet (above, Musée Granet, Aix-en-Provence), conceived in the early days of the romantic movement, has a classical air, enhanced by the architectural background of the Trinità dei Monti, thought by some to have been painted by the sitter, himself a landscape artist, rather than by Ingres. Few men have left as definite a mark on the taste of their time as Robert de Montesquiou (opposite), beautiful as a clean-shaven youth, supremely elegant with his upturned moustaches in middle age. Boldini painted him holding in his gloved hand a favourite cane into which he had had inserted a jewel once in the possession of Louis XIV. (Musée Jacquemart-André)

Heroes appear in many guises, but few are as decorative as St George (opposite), in Pisanello's great picture which shows him conversing with St Anthony (National Gallery). The warrior-saint is clad in white armour with the most splendid of all wide-brimmed hats on his blond head. Today's heroes are less spectacularly attired, though the many decorations and orders of Earl Mountbatten's uniform make a splendid foil to his severe but unusually handsome features (photograph reproduced by courtesy of Earl Mountbatten). A predecessor in valour and fame was the great Duke of Wellington whose alert face, as painted by Goya (National Gallery, London) has an air of determination which gives a clue to his extraordinary character. Heroes of the seventeenth century were incommoded both by plate armour and the long-haired wig of the period. Murrough O'Brien, courageous soldier and successful statesman, created Earl of Inchiquin by Charles I for his loyalty to the royal cause, wears both these cumbersome accoutrements together with a fall of lawn at the throat and a sash at the waist. (Portrait by J. M. Wright, City Art Gallery, Manchester.

HEROES

DANCERS

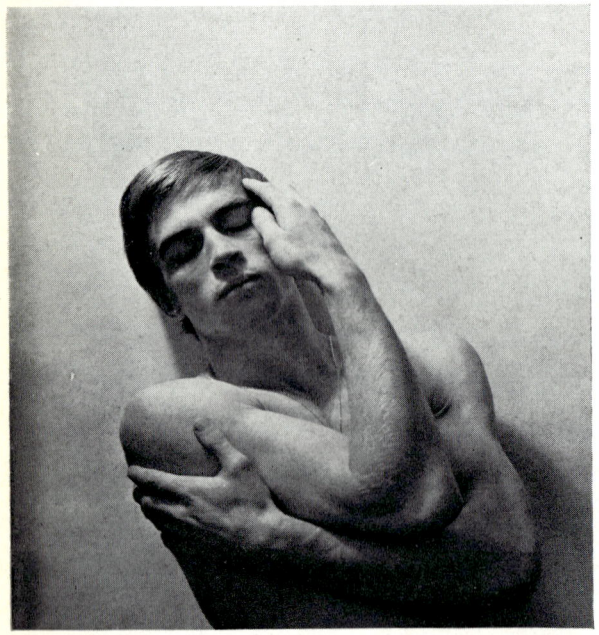

The male dancer has become increasingly admired in the twentieth century. The favourites of the nineteenth century tended to be women; but just before the First World War Nijinsky created a legend which persists today. In more recent times Serge Lifar's glamorous personality, sustained by his real good looks as well as his astounding performances, made him the great success of the 'thirties, when Cecil Beaton took this dramatic photograph of him (left) in *Ecossaise*. The greatest Russian dancer to emerge since Nijinsky is undoubtedly Nureyev (lower left), about whose personal appearance many disagree, some thinking him too animal in his approach and expression, others finding in him the apotheosis of masculine looks. Cecil Beaton's photograph stresses both his muscular strength and his mysterious quality of belonging to another world. One of the Royal Ballet's stars today is Donald MacCleary (opposite), who made his first great success at Covent Garden in '59 in *Swan Lake*. He is the epitome of the romantic ballet dancer, and his Prince Florimund in *The Sleeping Beauty* is a supremely poetical performance. (Photo, Zoe Dominic)

THE LOOK OF THE 'TWENTIES

Between the wars taste favoured the non-committal gentleman, recognisable by his moderation in all things; profiles were good but not Grecian, hair thick but not curly, and above all sleeked back, well cut and well brushed. Clothes and manners were in impeccable style, though the celebrated accompanist Ivor Newton once remarked that the Prince of Wales' smooth fair hair and fresh complexion (above left) irresistibly reminded him of the music-hall artist Vesta Tilley, known for her impersonations of the smart young man about town. Even Ivor Novello's gazelle good looks (above right), the antithesis of Nordic restraint, were subdued to the prevalent good taste, though his stage performances in such

Ruritanian surroundings as those of *Careless Rapture* gave endless scope for a more glamorous presentation.

Into this drawing-room world the cinema brought the man of action, the buccaneering Douglas Fairbanks, the cowboy bravado of William Hart, and the Gallic gaiety of Maurice Chevalier (above left). The singer wears his sailor hat at a jaunty angle and sports a bow-tie, then considered rather 'fast', but he, of course, could be excused because he was French. Owen Nares (far right) was typical of the blue-eyed young Englishman, clean and healthy, and his soulful rendering of the celibate clergyman faced with the allurements of Doris Keane in the aptly termed play *Romance* brought tears to the eyes of all who saw him. (Photographs: the Prince of Wales, Radio Times Hulton Picture Library; Ivor Novello, the Mander and Mitchenson Collection; Maurice Chevalier, Camera Press; Owen Nares, the Victoria and Albert Enthoven Collection)

THE 'THIRTIES

The biter bitten: above is Cecil Beaton looking at his own reflection in the mirror he holds in front of him, together with some roses, photographed by his friend and mentor, George Hoyningen-Huene. Robert Harris (right) early showed his love and aptitude for the theatre when at Oxford he played in the O.U.D.S. production of Thomas Hardy's *Dynasts*. His favourite parts have included 'Richard II' and Marlow's 'Faustus' but those who have followed his career found his interpretation of *The Matter of J. Robert Oppenheimer* one of his most moving performances. (Portrait painted in 1933 by Kenneth Green)

Cary Grant (right), whose sleek hair and handsome face always have been considered typically English, made his first Hollywood hit with Mae West in *She Done Him Wrong* in 1932, and followed this success by playing opposite Marlene Dietrich in *Blonde Venus* (photo, Clarence S. Bull, Kobal collection). Johnnie Weissmuller (far right) became as famous for his ungentlemanly behaviour as the English actor for his good manners, and during most of the 'thirties played 'Tarzan' with unfailing zest, uprooting trees and holding female bodies in the palm of his hand with consummate ease. In the 'forties he took on human shape in the person of 'Jungle Jim', a white hunter. (Photo, Cecil Beaton)

If the faces of the 'sixties are unconventional in features it is because the individual is more important than the type, and the anti-hero is the hero of today. In this new style Mick Jagger (above) is outstandingly successful. He formed in '62 the group entitled 'The Rolling Stones', who play guitars, pianos, harps and harpsichords at will, and he has been their chief star and vocalist ever since, writing his own music and words, sometimes in conjunction with Keith Richard. He is the southern answer to the pop-group menace from the midlands and the north, for he was born in Dartford, Kent, and now, aged twenty-five, lives in Chelsea with Marianne Faithfull, who played Ophelia in the recent much-praised *Hamlet* at the Round House. (Photo, Cecil Beaton)

FACES OF THE 'SIXTIES

Patrick Lichfield (above, self-portrait) has stepped out of line and is known as a world-famous photographer rather than Lord Lichfield. His sense of fun, of timing and of character, plus an unexpected efficiency, has made him the chosen recorder of many places and people for a variety of newsprint, glossy and otherwise. The only pity is that he is so often at the wrong end of the camera. Terence Stamp (left), once equated with Marlon Brando, and of the same generation as the Beatles, found a philosophy of love which has led him to write a novel as well as make a psychological Western called *Blue*. Here he is seen, tired and defiant, surrounded by the high white grass of the Utah plains. (Photo, Lawrence Schiller, Camera Press)

Le danger du tête à tête. Engraving by J. B. Simonet, after Baudouin

The Art of Seduction

BY JAMES LAVER

REMY DE GOURMONT in that disconcerting book of his *La Physique de l'Amour* tells us of a certain kind of spider of which the female is twenty times the size of the male and devours her mate in the very act of intercourse. The praying mantis is said to have similar disagreeable habits, eating her lover *in situ* from the head downwards. Not much place for the art of seduction here! But for the greater part of creation the situation is very different. Every spring 'a livelier iris changes on the burnished dove', and we have all watched the slightly ludicrous comedy of the courtship of pigeons.

The basic pattern is quite simple: the female pretends to run away and the male pursues her, prancing and swelling out his feathers in an effort, endlessly renewed, to attract attention. He is the very picture of the *marcheur* of the Paris boulevards during *la belle Époque*.

Enough of ornithology! Let us turn to man, who alas! has no feathers to ruffle, no crest to erect, no peacock's tail to spread; but he still pursues the female of his species and in the course of this pursuit employs every device that his fertile fancy can suggest. We are not here concerned with the feathers in his hair or the necklace of lion's teeth round his neck. We are concerned with his behaviour, his gestures, in a word his manners, his way of approaching his desired mate.

Such manners have varied enormously from age to age. The old joke about the manners and customs of primitive man: 'manners none, customs nasty', must have held good for the greater part of prehistory if not of history itself. Marriage by capture, for instance, can never have offered much scope for the niceties of *galanterie*. And for some of the historic civilisations there was no question of any art of seduction. You simply went to a marriage-broker who approached the parents of a suitable young woman and, after a lot of haggling over the dowry, a deal was concluded, 'a marriage was arranged'. The young man had very little say in the matter and the young woman none at all.

Of course, *outside* marriage there was plenty of scope for sexual adventure with mere common prostitutes or with the most cultivated *hetairae*, but in this situation there was no need for the man to seduce the woman; she seduced him. It is not until women have attained at least a certain degree of emancipation that it is necessary to *court* them, to behave, that is, as a courtier trying to obtain a favour from a king, and in order to do this it is necessary to be *courteous*, to make oneself agreeable. In order to solicit a favour it is essential to be favourably received.

One does not solicit favours from inferiors, and therefore, so long as woman is regarded as a mere chattel, there can be no question of the art of seduction. The woman must be *in some way* in a superior position, in a position to *grant* favours, and it is generally admitted that the first time this happened in history was in Western Europe in the early Middle Ages. The peculiar institution of feudalism brought it about that a *grande dame* had many young men about her who, although of noble birth themselves, were, in fact, her servants. They had entered her husband's service as pages or whatever they might be called. Hence the double meaning of the word 'mistress', a meaning which would have been incomprehensible in the Ancient World.

Much has been written about 'courtly love', and it was plain from the beginning that it had nothing to do with the relationship between the baron and his chatelaine—another revealing word—the lady who kept the castle. The marriage itself had been arranged on the good old principle of worldly advantage. A 'good marriage' was one which increased the size of the fief. Courtly love could only exist between the lady—the *domina*—and the young men who approached her with bows and genuflections. The idea of the 'lady' had been born, with the most profound consequences for the whole climate of sensibility in the West. For woman had been put on a pedestal and if, in the beginning, it was only the lady of the château who benefited, the idea gradually filtered down to all but the lower reaches of society until, in our own day, the word lady has been so widely applied (the charlady and 'Mr Cochran's Young Ladies') that it has ceased to have any meaning at all.

The chief exponents of courtly love were, of course, the

troubadours, and much ink has been spilled in the endeavour to decide who exactly they were and what they were up to. They might not owe allegiance to any particular lady; they proclaimed themselves the servants of 'the Lady' as such. They sang her praises in poems of the most extraordinary formal complexity. They organised Courts of Love (although this is disputed by some scholars) in which the most delicate and subtle questions were debated. In a word, they invented Romantic Love.

Such love, they maintained, was impossible between husband and wife. It could only exist in adultery, but it was an adultery of a peculiar kind, for, in the poems themselves, no physical love-making is ever implied. The lover pleaded and the lady always said 'no'. Whether she always said 'no' in practice is another question, and no doubt there was often an element of hypocrisy, or at least of make-believe, in the sentiments expressed. There was also a lot of nonsense; but at least the troubadour-idea constituted a school of manners. Courtesy between men and women became the accepted ideal even if such an ideal was rarely realised.

The troubadours were almost all Cathars, that is to say, heretics, and in the Albigensian Crusade the Provençal civilisation in which they had flourished was totally destroyed. But their ideas had spread abroad all over Europe, to reappear in the most unlikely places. There is a sense in which Dante himself is their heir. No one put woman on a higher pedestal than he, finally almost identifying Beatrice with the Holy Wisdom itself.

All this, no doubt, was far removed from the actual relationship between men and women in the Italian Renaissance; but whatever refinement of manners there was can be traced back to the troubadours and to the attitude to women which they had inaugurated. Indeed it is difficult to see how the high position women had attained by the sixteenth century would have been possible without it. Not all women, of course, but if the sixteenth century is notable for anything it is surely for the astonishing number of Great Ladies it produced, from Isabella d'Este to Queen Elizabeth I. Certainly the high-born women of the period (and some not so high-born, as for example Margaret Roper, daughter of Sir Thomas More) were as well educated as

The Art of Seduction

their male contemporaries, and were able to converse with them on equal terms. The art of seduction, one feels, must have been practised at this time on a very high intellectual level.

The wars of religion, culminating in the Thirty Years War, and the Great Rebellion in England, cannot have contributed to a refinement of manners, but by the end of the seventeenth century things had settled down again. The wars of the eighteenth century were no longer essays in genocide, or attempts to exterminate religious dissidents; they had become the marching and countermarching of professional armies in pursuit of dynastic ambitions. The opposing armies did not fight in the winter months. They 'went into winter quarters' and the officers at least returned to their respective capitals to enjoy themselves before the opening of the spring campaign. War, in a word, had dwindled into a kind of game.

Now, it has recently been maintained (notably by Denis de Rougemont in his *Passion and Society*) that there is a close correlation between the way men make war and the way they make love. In the eighteenth century the capture of a city did not mean the destruction of that city as it would today. It might be called a rape, but it could not be called a murder. Even rape is too strong a word, for the surrender was often arranged by negotiation. And the victorious besiegers gave parties and balls and danced with the ladies who had been besieged.

So love itself became a kind of game, with the strictest rules of punctilio, and the art of seduction was pushed to new heights of formality and polish. In fact one feels that the eighteenth-century lover loved 'the game beyond the prize'. Seduction became a kind of fencing match with buttons on the foils.

It was no longer a question of putting woman on a pedestal. The eighteenth-century gallant would have found the sentiments of the troubadours incomprehensible. The scene had been shifted from the court and the castle to the boudoir and salon. Women were no longer on a pedestal but on the same parquet floor in a room decorated by Boucher or Carlo van Loo. At no other period of history has seduction been conducted with so much decorum.

This was not only true of the highest ranks of society. James

Boswell, for all that he was the Laird of Auchinleck, hardly belonged to *that*. Yet he records in his diary an affair he had with a young actress named Louisa Lewis. As Morton M. Hunt points out (in his admirable book *The Natural History of Love*) 'he copied down his own conversation as faithfully as he later did Samuel Johnson's', and so 'we have a chance to eavesdrop upon him and hear the very words an eighteenth-century gallant and a lady spoke'.

BOSWELL: I hope you will not be so cruel as to keep me in misery. (*He begins to take some liberties.*)
MRS LEWIS: Nay, Sir—now—but do consider—
BOSWELL: Ah, Madame!
MRS LEWIS: Nay, but you are an encroaching creature! (*He deftly lifts up her petticoats*) Good heaven, Sir!
BOSWELL: Madame, I cannot help it, I adore you. Do you like me?
MRS LEWIS (*kissing him*): O Mr Boswell!
BOSWELL (*still struggling against her resistance*): But my dear Madame! Permit me, I beseech you.

Boswell duly succeeded with the lady, but alas! shortly afterwards he realised that she had transmitted to him a venereal disease. He taxed her with it.

MRS LEWIS: Sir, you have terrified me. I protest I know nothing of the matter.
BOSWELL: I give you my word of honour that you shall not be discovered.
MRS LEWIS: Sir, this is being more generous than I could expect.
BOSWELL: I hope, Madame, you will own that since I have been with you, I have always behaved like a man of honour.
MRS LEWIS: You have indeed, Sir.
BOSWELL (*rising*): Madame, your most obedient servant.

Nothing could be more formal and correct; and yet nothing could be further from *l'amour courtois*. Denis de Rougemont (to quote again from that remarkable book of his) remarks that 'woman in the eyes of men of the eighteenth century was merely an object. At one extreme there had been the ideal woman, the unalloyed symbol of a Love drawing love away beyond visible forms; at the other there was now woman as a mere means to pleasure, the more or less agreeable instrument of a sensation which kept men self-isolated.' And he notes that 'from about the time Louis the Fourteenth died in 1715 till Louis the Sixteenth ascended the throne in 1774, Don Juan reigned over the dreams of a French aristocracy that had gradually fallen from feudal heroism'. Fallen indeed! for there is precious little difference between a Duc de Richelieu and an adventurer like Casanova. One wonders sometimes if either was really interested in the women he seduced. What interested them both was the art of seduction.

Perhaps the flavour of the period is distilled most completely in *Les Liaisons Dangereuses*, Choderlos de Laclos' masterpiece. It is perhaps the most heartless book ever written. It is cynicism to a quintessential degree, and there can be little doubt that it represents the prevailing climate of the court of Louis XV.

And yet, almost contemporary with it, is another book, Richardson's *Pamela*, which represents a very different climate. On the one hand cynicism *à l'outrance*; on the other sentiment dissolving into *sensiblerie*, and there can be little doubt which was to gain the upper hand for the rest of the eighteenth century and for the whole course of the Romantic Movement. Once more woman is put upon a pedestal; once more man yearns for the unattainable; once more the whole point of 'love' is that it does not find satisfaction on the physical plane. A 'credibility gap' opens between passion and performance; and the hero and heroine of Benardin de St Pierre not only do not consummate their love but prefer to drown rather than see one another naked. In the pictorial arts the frank eroticism of Boucher has given place to the sentimentality of Greuze.

Of course there was a lot of nonsense about the romanticism of the late eighteenth and early nineteenth centuries. In practice Byron behaved just as badly as Casanova, and 'Prinny' was just as lascivious as Louis XV. None the less the prevailing sentiment did have an effect on manners, although whether the result would satisfy the requirements of a strict morality is another matter. What had really happened was that women were once more divided into two categories: respectable women and —the rest. It is one of the ironies of social history that when we speak of a 'moral age' we mean an age in which there is more prostitution than promiscuity. The nineteenth century as a whole fell into this category and, as we have already remarked, when dealing with prostitutes there is no need to practise the art of seduction.

That art flourished again towards the close of the century, in *la belle Époque*. One has only to glance at Paul Bourget's *Physiologie de l'Amour Moderne*, or even at the anonymous *Comment Seduire Les Femmes* which appeared at the same time, to realise as much. Adultery with women of one's own social class was once more the mode, although the cynicism involved was perhaps less overt than in the eighteenth century.

How very different in our modern age! As Yvonne Cloud once remarked, the great discovery of our time is that 'girls like it too'. Men sometimes found this disappointing, and a modern versifier was moved to protest:

> Don't be too easy, Baby!
> I want to yearn for you.
> I want to flutter round
> Like the moth to the flame.
> I want to work out
> All the rules of the game.
> I want to go slow,
> I want to imagine
> All the things I don't know.
>
> Don't be in a hurry
> To give me your lips.
> Love's just a worry
> When it once comes to grips.
> Don't swim with the stream,
> Just be my dream,
> For to my dream I'm true,
> Don't be too easy, Baby!
> I want to yearn for you.
>
> Be a little hard to please
> And difficult to understand.
> Only on my bended knees
> Give me leave to kiss your hand.
> Let me falter, make me woo,
> Learn to say your lover 'No'!

> Lest the proverb prove too true,
> Easy come and easy go.
> Don't be too easy, Baby
> I want to yearn for you.

But, in the 'twenties and 'thirties and since, there cannot have been many who shared such sentiments. Seduction, if it can be called so, has become a very simple matter: a drink, a dinner, 'Can I take you home'. Yet there has been one amusing change in technique since I was young. Young men, it seems, no longer say: 'Come up and see my etchings'. They say: 'Come up and hear my L.Ps.' Marshall McLuhan might have something to say to that.

L'épouse indiscrète. Engraving by N. de Launay, after Baudouin, 1771

INDISCRETION I: BEFORE
BY WILLIAM HOGARTH

THE PAIR of paintings reproduced above is by William Hogarth. Now known as 'Indiscretion 1' and 'Indiscretion 2', the paintings are believed to have been known in the eighteenth century as 'Before' and 'After'. They should not be confused with a pair of engravings by Hogarth, with these same titles, which depict the seducer and his victim in a bedroom.

INDISCRETION II: AFTER
BY WILLIAM HOGARTH

IT IS BELIEVED that William Hogarth painted this pair of paintings in 1730 or 1731. Each canvas measures approximately $14\frac{1}{2}$ by $17\frac{1}{2}$ inches. They were for many years in private ownership, and were presented in 1964 to the Fitzwilliam Museum, Cambridge. They are now reproduced, in colour for the first time, by courtesy of the Syndics of the Fitzwilliam Museum.

La toilette. Engraving by Nicolas Ponce, after Baudouin, 1771

Arts of Attraction

BY RAYMOND LAMONT BROWN

THOUSANDS of years ago woman found out that her face is only her fortune as long as it is attracting interest. Every proprietor of a modern chemist's shop will tell you that without the cosmetic department the profit turnover would be drastically cut. Today the cosmetic industry is vast in its volume and ramifications.

In all probability cosmetics had their origin amongst the aristocracy of Ancient China, although primitive peoples have always painted their bodies to ward off the perils of war, evil spirits and illness, and for the enhancement of beauty in courtship. For the earliest source of records on this subject one must turn to the Egypt of the Pharaohs, for the 'painted men' in prehistoric cave murals were not using cosmetics. Among the remains of the First and Thinite dynasty of Egypt, *circa* 3200 B.C., toilet articles and unguent receptacles have been found. Certain bowls thought to contain ointments have been found at similar sites dating some five hundred years earlier.

Make-up was very important in the daily social life of Ancient Egypt and women took great care in choosing shades of powder and paint to match their particular complexions. It was fashionable to smear the face with white paste, made up from a rather dubious mixture of flour and poisonous white lead. To this was added the fragrances of myrrh, frankincense and spikenard, and a coating of sesame, almond and olive oils.

A substance called kohl, made from antimony, was much used by Egyptian women. It was applied with ivory or wooden spatulae. Thyme, origanum and balanus (often called acorn shells) were used in a powder form. When Howard Carter opened the Tomb of Tutankhamen he found cosmetic jars with contents still smelling of an elusive fragrance even after the passing of three thousand years.

The Egyptians considered the eyes to be the most important part of the face and continually reproduced the eye shape on amulets. Painting the under-side of the eye green and the lids, lashes and eyebrows black with the application of kohl gave an exotic look and was similar to the 'Kookie' look recently favoured by modern girls. The dark eyes were complemented by an orange crayon; finger- and toenails were enhanced with a dark grey antimony powder and lengthened in Arabesque fashion as a symbol of clairvoyance.

Henna dyed the finger-nails and the palms of feet; the menfolk of distinction added thick creams to their faces and a postiche, or false beard, the length of which determined their rank.

Archaeologists are continually bringing to light the beautiful ivory, onyx, porphyry and alabaster pots, jars and boxes which contained the Egyptian cosmetics and which graced the dressing-stools of both men and women. Most, if not all, of the early cosmetics were made by the priests, after time-honoured and mysterious arts and recipes. A careful regard of the graffiti on such monuments as the Sphinx of Thutmoses IV, *circa* 1420 B.C., shows how early offerings of fragrant oils and make-up were made to the Gods of Ancient Egypt.

The Babylonians and the Hebrews also knew of cosmetics, the former using ground pumice and the latter powdered gold as an adornment, but both used a little eye make-up. The Jews used rouge, powder for hair and a number of vegetable dyes, although the Mishna forbade the use of rouge on the Sabbath, and women who used powder made of flour for make-up were solemnly charged to remove it at the time of the Passover.

Most religious manuscripts make some mention of cosmetics. The Koran, Sura IVI, states: 'And theirs shall be the Houris with *large dark eyes*, like pearls hidden in their shells.' From time to time the Bible comments on the use of cosmetics. II Kings ix, 30: 'And when Jehu was come to Jezreel, Jezebel heard of it; and she painted her face, and tired her head, and looked out at a window.' Jeremiah iv, 30: 'And when thou art spoiled, what wilt thou do? Though thou clothest thyself with crimson, though thou deckest thee with ornaments of gold, though thou rentest thy face with painting, in vain shalt thou make thyself fair; thy lovers will despise thee, they will seek thy life.' Ezekiel xxiii, 40: '... for whom thou didst wash thyself, paintedst thy eyes, and deckedst thyself with ornaments.'

The mirrors and toilet articles used by Aztec women were very similar to those used by women of other early civilisations, pyrites and obsidian being used for such articles. Aztec women favoured a yellow tint for their naturally brown-bronzed skins and used widely a cream called *axin*, for dazzling complexions, and an earthy substance of yellow colour called *tecozauitl*. Staining teeth black and red was a practice of the foremost beauties among the Huaxtecs and the Otami. Women in almost all periods of Aztec civilisation painted their arms and breasts with delicate blue patterns, finishing off their personal freshness by chewing *tzictli*.

In ancient Byzantium there were apparently no cosmetics, although in Homeric Greece, while rouge was lacking, false hair and vegetable dyes were used. Most women in Ancient Greece persisted with their creams and oils although their lovers protested that the heat produced sweat, '. . . and the sweat produces red streaks on your cheeks and neck; and when your hair touches your face it gets dirty with white paint'.

The Roman woman of early times showed little enthusiasm for facial adornment and it was only after some contact with the Greeks that they did much with the aesthetic side of their personal appearance. The importance of cosmetics came during the reign of Nero, who himself used cosmetics lavishly, as did his wife Poppaea. The art of make-up in Rome was called *cultus* and included the use of scents, *mundus*, and jewellery, *ornatus*. Writers like Ovid wrote pages about the way in which a face should be made up. In his *Medicamina faciei femineae*—'On making-up a woman's face'—he gives several suitable prescriptions. One unguent was made up of a mixture of eggs, ground antlers, gum, barley, powdered pulse, narcissus bulbs, honey and wheat flour. Perfumes mostly came from the East, or from the local Italian centre of Capua market, Seplasia.

Not all Roman men allowed themselves to be seduced by a pretty made-up face; the writer Lucian was one:

> If you saw women getting out of bed in the morning, you would find them more repulsive than monkeys. That is why they shut themselves up and refuse to be seen by a man; old hags and a troupe of servants as ugly as

Arts of Attraction 68

their mistresses surround her, plastering her unhappy face with a variety of medicaments. For a woman does not just wash away her sleepiness with cold water, and proceed to a serious day's work. No, innumerable concoctions in the way of salves are used to brighten her unpleasing complexion. As in a public procession, each of the servants has some different object in her hand; a silver basin, a jug, a mirror, a multitude of boxes, enough to stock a chemist's shop, jars full of mischief, tooth powders or stuff for blackening the eyelids.

Rome had no chemists' shops as such, but the *Pharmacopola*—drug-sellers—mixed concoctions in an unlicensed way. The charlatan hawked his wares and the *Unguentarii, Pigmentarii, Turarii, Seplasarii,* and *Aromatarii,* did a roaring trade in white lead, *cerussa,* chalk, frangipani, *fucus* (a sort of rouge), and *psilotrum* (a kind of depilatory); barley flour and butter were particularly mixed as a cure for acne. *Cumin* gave the face a porcelain and interesting look, likewise the flax seed improved the complexion and made the nails bright and smooth. The breath was kept fresh with a mixture of barley, salt and honey, which also made the teeth whiter. Laurel leaves chewed after drinking were enough to fool censorious wives, while a concoction of boiled leek roots, drunk, prevented 'B.O.'.

Modern man looks sadly on baldness as a sign of age and resigns himself to it. The flower of Roman manhood, however, had a constant horror of going bald. In a dire attempt to arrest his steadily receding locks he was led to seek out every sort of remedy. He would consult the cosmetics quacks and be supplied with a formula, in exchange for a few *denarii*, to suit the texture of his head. One formula was in the form of a hair cream and was manufactured out of maidenhair cooked in celery seeds and oil; this was made into a paste and applied to the hair, which was supposed to become thick and curly.

For the partial falling out of hair and the general greying of colour the following was recommended: 'Take thou soda and rub thy head with it. Next apply a mixture of wine, saffron and pepper. Finally a paste of vinegar, laserpicium and rat dung.' You might have kept your hair with such a mixture, but certainly not your friends!

The Roman Emperor Augustine always made a special point

of using a different perfume for each part of his body—mint for under the arms, palm oil for the chest and essence of ivy for the backs of the knees. The bottles and jars on a Roman citizen's dressing-table were generally divided into three sections: *Ledysmata*—for solid unguents, *Stymmata*—for liquid unguents, and *Diapasmata*—for perfumes and powders. About the middle of the Roman Empire's glory cultured women were spending more time at their toilet and it became true that even though women were made before mirrors they were before them ever after.

White skin was a sign of great beauty in Japan and a mark of aristocratic birth. Japanese artists of ancient times always made a special point of making the skins of high-ranking persons appear to be of a lighter texture. Japanese women applied a very generous amount of white chalk to their faces, only seen nowadays among the *geisha*, with a little bright rouge for a rose-button mouth. They also plucked their eyebrows and blackened their teeth with a dye made from powdered gallnut and vinegar, or tea. Nowadays cosmetic trends in Japan tend to follow the ways of the West.

In India beauty was thought to go hand in hand with good character, and cosmetics became widely used by both men and women. The range of cosmetics was from common products to very costly preparations, the main ones being *rhus venicifera*, a resin used for staining feet and the palms of hands, sticks of sandalwood, myrrh and various essences refined from cinnamon, saffron and ginger. The perfumers, *gandhika*, spent most of their time around the entrances to bath houses and did a particularly brisk trade in pills for bad breath and powdered camphor, musk, cardamom and cloves mixed with mango-juice. A body sweetener was made of nard, saffron, gum-benjamin, pine resin, sandalwood, myrrh and holy water. Eyes were penned with *añjana*, and different types of cosmetic recipes were used for coquetry, religious ritual and sexual acts, household duties and the general desire to please.

'Lipstick' is a comparatively modern word but crayons or eye-pencils are very old in origin. They were made mainly from alabaster calcinate or a base of a type of plaster of Paris, rolled into paste sticks and dried in the sun.

Arts of Attraction

The *Kama Sutra* of Vatsyayana was particularly explicit on cosmetics:

> An ointment made of the fruit of the embilica myrabolans soaked in the milky juice of the milk hedge plant, of the soma plant, the calotropis gigantea, and the juice of the fruit of the vernonia anthemintica, will make the hair white. . . .
> The colour of the lips can be regained by means of the madayantica. . . .
> If water be mixed with oil and ashes of any kind of grass except the kusha grass, it becomes the colour of milk. . . .
> If a fine powder is made of tabernamontana coronaria, the costus speciosus or arabicus and the flacourtia cataphracta, and applied to the wick of a lamp, which is made to burn with the oil of blue vitriol, the black pigment or lampblack produced therefrom, when applied to the eyelids has the effect of making a person look lovely. . . .
> The oil of the hogweed, the echites putescens, the sarina plant, the yellow amaranth, and the leaf of the nymphae, if applied to the body, has the same effect. . . .

The Indian young man of fashion chewed betel-nut quids in the bath and then vigorously rubbed his teeth with root. After washing with *phenaka*—a kind of perfumed soapy substance—the chest was powdered with camphorated talcum and the young man painted a decorative mark on his forehead with red *arsenic* and drew good-luck signs on his arms with civet paste. Red-lac on the lips contrasted with black eyelids and mango was chewed before venturing out.

After bathing a princess her personal maids massaged her with gum from roots (the maids had to chew lemon aloes all the time they were with the princess so that they did not infect the air with their inferiority). Once she was properly massaged the princess's hair was dried and black incense was brushed through it. The maids rubbed paste of ground sandalwood into her body and smeared musk-scented saffron over her breasts and feet, painting the soles of her feet with lac. Her body was then tinted with aromatic dyes of red, white, black and green, and her nipples were specially tinted with a paste of coral.

Collyrium was favoured for the eyes, and *aśmarāga*—orange-coloured mineral powder—for the lips. The beauty spot *tilaka* was then affixed on the forehead. Although there are links between ancient religious sites of Mohenjodaro and Sumer, Indian monks and priests were forbidden cosmetics.

In Europe the whims of monarchs have been a decisive factor as to whether cosmetics were used or not in a particular age. Louis XIII of France was greatly enamoured of their use; therefore cosmetics flourished during his reign. But Louis XIV did not favour them, so they almost died out at court, to come back again on his death to a climax of *Poudre à la Marèchale* in Napoleon's time.

Whatever the age there have always been people who opposed the use of cosmetics. Religious documents and pamphlets are dotted with broadsides against people who used cosmetics. In the eighteenth century a bill was introduced into the English Parliament stating:

> ... that women of whatever age, rank, profession, or degree, whether virgins, maids, or widows, that shall from and after each Act, impose upon, seduce, and betray into matrimony, any of His Majesty's subjects, by the scents, paints, cosmetic washes, artificial teeth, false hair, Spanish wool [a wool impregnated with carmine], iron stays, hoops, high heeled shoes, bolstered hips, shall incur the penalty of the law in force against witchcraft and like misdemeanours and that the marriage, upon conviction, shall be null and void.

Such a law was enforced in the State of Pennsylvania; and generally cosmetics were frowned upon in the Colonies, especially Puritan New England. One can go back even further, to the time of the Incas, and read a father's advice to his daughter:

> Listen to me, child; never make up your face nor paint it; never put red on your mouth to look beautiful; make-up and paint are things that light women use—shameless creatures. If you want your husband to love you, dress well, wash yourself and wash your clothes.

The history of cosmetics in Great Britain is spread over about a thousand years. Several samples of toilet articles were brought back by the Crusaders, picked up after some had dallied in a harem or two. It was reported at this time that 'Moorish women cover their faces with black cypress bespotted with lead ... tattoo their faces by pricking the skin and rubbing it over with ink and the juice of a herb. . . .' During the early Middle Ages the cosmetics used in this country were similar to those of Ancient Rome but without the great variety of choice and certainly without the overture of the bath. Later in the period came a little paint and dyes, with a small number of perfumes. The Anglo-Saxons used only a little blue hair powder and had painted cheeks. Apparently the people of the later Middle Ages did not favour cosmetics, but by 1300 they were using a little saffron and perfume.

Although bleached hair and plucked eyebrows became the fashion in the fourteenth century, the fifteenth century produced little or no cosmetics. The sixteenth century brought perfume to both men and women, and a night-mask of oil became popular. By the reign of Queen Elizabeth I many perfumed substances were the fashion, mainly as a relief from the terrible stench which came from the sewers, and ladies carried around 'sweet coffers' attached to their belts. The ladies of the court painted their faces, necks and breasts with a lead vermilion said to have been introduced by Catherine de Medici. Belladonna used by the Venetian woman came to England and was used to dilate the pupils, and still several women bit their lips to redden them. It is said that Mary Queen of Scots favoured a cosmetic bath of French red wine, but the initiative for such exotic tastes had been taken over a thousand years before by Cleopatra.

For the most part cosmetics were confined to the towns, country lasses usually relying on the fresh air to enrich their complexions. Shakespeare, being himself a countryman, was intrigued by the use of cosmetics and made mention of the practices in his sonnets and plays. One finds in the opening scene of the third Act of *Hamlet* the Prince saying to Ophelia: 'I have heard of your paintings too, well enough; God has given you one face, and you make yourselves another.'

The seventeenth century was certainly one in which great respect was paid to cosmetics by both men and women, and while paint and powder were widely used, patches became all the rage. Perhaps the patch, as a facial decoration, deserves a history of its own, for it is nearly as old as perfumery and paint. Several small boxes unearthed at the decimated city of Pompeii, destroyed by the eruption of Mount Vesuvius in A.D. 79, would suggest that Roman ladies were in the habit of sticking small pieces of cloth and paper on their faces as a form of beauty culture. The patch, or 'tâche-noir', probably came to England around 1616, when the play *Comedie of Pasquil and Katherine* was being played, for one of the characters remarks: '... even as black patches are worne, some for pride and some to stay the rheume'.

Bulwer, the Puritan writer, leaves us a more cogent account:

> Our ladies have entertained a vague custom of spotting their faces out of affectation of a mole to set off their beauty, such as Venus had, and it is well if one black patch will serve to make faces remarkable, for some fill their visages full of them, varied into all manner of shapes and figures.

The shape of the patch took on many marks of ingenuity; ships, windmills, flowers and even coaches-and-four were used as silhouette designs, and very often ladies showed their political allegiances by the patches they wore. Tory supporters wore a patch on the left, the Whigs on the right side of the face.

The language of the patch became as involved as that of the fan. A teasing coquette would place her patch near her lip, the correct corner being the left-hand side of the upper lip. But the girl who wished to convey deeper and more lasting feelings would wear a round or heart-shaped patch on the left-hand corner of the eyelid. Placed below the eye the patch meant friendship only.

Several men added patches to their cosmetics in order to cover old battle scars. The famous portrait of the Earl of Arlington, wounded at Naseby, painted by Lely, shows milord with a piece of sticking plaster shaped to cover a scar on his nose. Again Reynolds' picture of Viscount Cathcart shows that nobleman with a large crescent-shaped patch under the eye to hide a wound received at Fontenoy.

The use of the patch was at its height at the close of the reign of Queen Anne, and dwindled after the coming of the House of Hanover. One of the reasons for patches eventually being forbidden was their treasonable use. Some ladies of Jacobite persuasion used their patches as secret signs that they supported 'the King o'er the water'.

In the latter part of the seventeenth century women had begun to use more white lead with a basis of Bear's Grease, rice, bismuth and quicksilver essence on their faces. These practices overlapped into the eighteenth century, and more men started to powder their hair; but even at this date little soap was used. The main ingredient of the rouges of the day was *cerusse*, a carbonate of lead, made by exposing plates of lead to the vapours of vinegar with a little red dye added.

By the early nineteenth century the patch had been discontinued and few men wore any make-up. Some dandies still persisted with a little rouge, but women favoured perfume to powder and lacquer.

By the early years of Victoria's reign the use of cosmetics was a thing of the past for men, and apart from a little macassar oil for the hair men employed no sweet-smelling appendices to their fashions. In men's circles there was a steady building up of feeling against cosmetics as being unmanly and effeminate, an attitude that persisted almost to this day. Women of the mid years of Victoria's reign had their powder and paint, artificial ringlets, hair dye, lotions for making up the eyes and dentifrice, but by 1880 there was practically no make-up used.

The 1890s saw the recurrence of a little face powder but even in 1900 make-up was considered too 'worldly' for respectable middle-class dames.

The 1920s brought a steady awakening of the cosmetic industry, and the clouds of war had not long drifted away when two women, each in her individual way, began to dominate the cosmetic scene. Elizabeth Arden experimented with lanoline, benzoin, almond oils and hamamelis, while Helena Rubinstein started by using a cream which her mother had given her to protect the skin. Soon both women were manufacturing their wares in great quantities. Courtesans and actresses had never abandoned the use of make-up, but the early 1920s heralded a new cosmetic age for the modest girl and 'respectable' woman.

The 'vamp' movies did much to stimulate women's tastes in cosmetics. Beauty parlours became the vogue; lipstick, mascara, powder, cream, tissue blender, astringent, mud-packs, foam rinses and many exotic perfumes came on to the scene, although there was a little less rouge towards the end of the 1920s.

The next forty years were to produce more changes of fashion in cosmetic culture than the previous three thousand. The 1930s began with carmine lipstick, although the red colouring was less obvious. Nail polish too became a vogue in different hues. During the early 1940s scarcely any rouge was used, and the emphasis was on lipstick and nail polish. Care was taken to match dresses to make-up.

During the period 1947–50 there was still scarcely any rouge, though lips were emphasised and nails became brilliant and dark coloured. Delicate colours evolved around 1949. By 1952 creamy skin was made to emphasise a lightly, though brightly, coloured lipstick.

For the past hundred years or so men have fought shy of the idea of using cosmetics. But the trends are now changing, and with the power of modern advertising men are expected to spend something like £20,000,000 per year on cosmetics over the next few years. The range is almost as large as that for women: hair shampoos, pre-, foam- and after-shave lotions, medicated bath mats, soap with *male* (?) perfumes, herbally treated towels, roll-on deodorants, anti-perspirant sprays, face-masks, soothing eyepads, hair lacquer, hair creams—the list is almost endless. A full set of male cosmetics would cost around £30. The logical conclusion? Handbags for men!

Today the trends of women's cosmetics have taken on the features of a science. There is a marked trend today towards cosmetics of lighter tone and texture colours, with a greater accent on the eyes; and rouges have developed from pink blobs in the centre of the cheek to aids for facial contour building and highlighting with a lipstick of paler shade. The ultimate refinement is, in the words of one beauty consultant, to achieve, by skilful use of make-up, 'that un-made-up look'.

Love without Words

BY RODNEY ACKLAND

'Hey, you there! wake up! jump to it! stop thinking about the pictures!' bawled the drill sergeant. I gave a guilty start. It was my first day at a new school. I was ten years old. Soon it became a habit with him to pick on me during drill instruction. What he bawled was what he had bawled before; and he kept it up throughout the years of my schooldays when, one of a handful of boarders at a suburban grammar school, I received my education at three gorgeous palaces which reared—like Sin its Ugly Head—their dubious architectural splendours on both sides of the High Street, and at a fourth which squatted, self-effacing, crushed between vast shop fronts, a genuine, ancient, flea-pit Bioscope—and no less magical for that.

It was 1918 when I first went to the school, the year of Lillian and Dorothy Gish in *Hearts of the World*, Fanny Ward and Sessue Hayakawa in *The Cheat*, Charlie Chaplin in *Sunnyside*, and the conclusion of the Great World War. I stayed there—with the sergeant bawling at me as always—until, ceasing to be a school-boy, I was able to continue my education unhindered at a different row of palaces in a High Street nearer home. That was in 1924, the year of John Gilbert in *The Big Parade*, Carol Dempster and Neil Hamilton in *Isn't Life Wonderful*, Pola Negri in *Forbidden Paradise*, and God knows what world-staggering events which I didn't take in at the time and remember nothing about now.

Whether or not it was initially a shot in the dark on the part of the school sergeant, or whether he was able to divine what type of images my mind was filled with by the 'soppy' expression on my face, I don't know to this day. Certain it is that if I wasn't enjoying a private run-through in my mind's eye of, say, the climactic excitements—with the ride-to-the-rescue horsemen charging right out of the screen and over one's head—of *The Virgin of Stamboul*, then I would be riveted by a vision of the elegantly gloved hand of Norma Talmadge firing the revolver with which, in *The Sign on the Door*, she put a peremptory end to the well-laid plans of Lew Cody to seduce her teenage daughter,

[continued on page 85]

Norma Talmadge and Lew Cody in *The Sign on the Door*, 1921

Above: Theda Bara with William Shay in *Sin*, 1915
Opposite: Pola Negri in *Forbidden Paradise*, 1924
Below: Marie Prevost and Monte Blue in *The Marriage Circle*, 1923

Three aspects of the Great Lover of the Silent Film—Rudolph Valentino. Above, in *The Sheik*, 1924, he carries Agnes Ayres into his tent in the desert, and, opposite, flings her on the divan with a view to 'having his will of her', a scene which always 'brought down the house'. Below, with much more finesse, he makes love to Alice Terry in Rex Ingram's *Four Horsemen of the Apocalypse*, 1921.

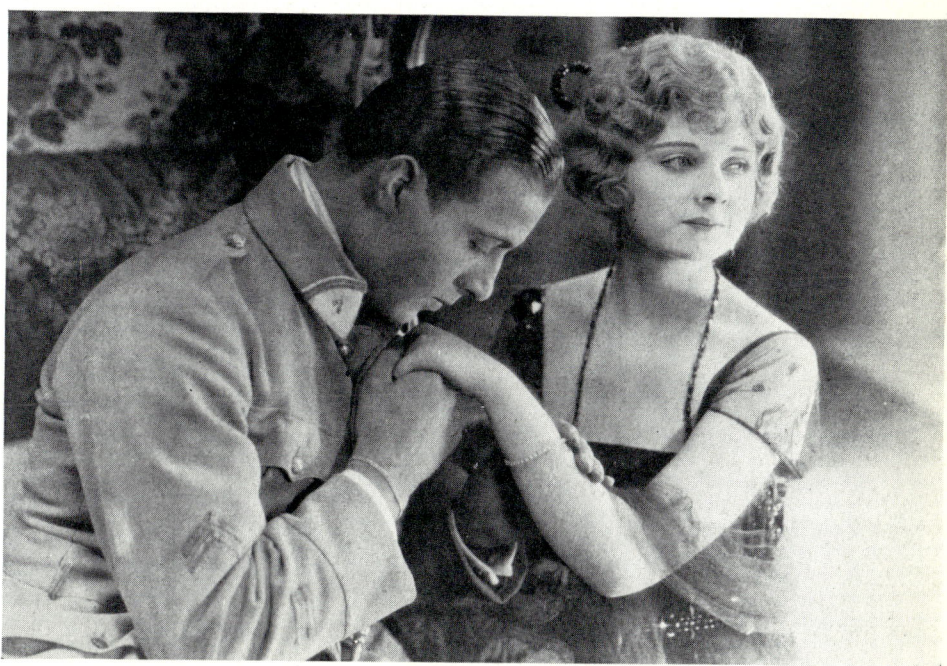

Mabel Normand with Wheeler Oakman in Mack Sennett's *Mickey*, 1918

Clara Bow with Antonio Moreno in *It*, 1927

Greta Garbo in *Joyless Street*, 1925

Dorothy Gish in D. W. Griffith's *Orphans of the Storm*, 1921

as twenty years and six reels previously, he had seduced *her*. Or I might be wishing I knew what the piece of music was which, lively but menacing, was so often played by the orchestra during duelling scenes (and which in later life I discovered to be the overture to *Figaro*); or, as a whole year or more used then to elapse before the general release of a film after its West End run, I might be counting the months, the weeks and finally the days in anticipation of that fortnight with 'Specially Augmented Orchestra' when, from the screen (foreverafter hallowed) of Pyke's Picture House, *Orphans of the Storm* would be decimating its audiences with pity and terror. ('Oh my godfathers!' the woman behind me kept moaning during the prolonged climax at the guillotine; '*Oh* my godfathers! *Oh* my godfathers!')

Then again, I might well be pondering over my never-to-be-told-about visit to the cinema with Miss Baines, the matron. She had been instructed to take me, convalescing after some youthful ailment, to see *With the Prince of Wales in India*, approved by the headmaster as suitable for schoolboys. We paused outside Pyke's Picture House, where Elinor Glyn's *The Career of Catherine Bush*, featuring Catherine Calvert, was on show. She ran her eye over the posters, had a quick look at the stills, glanced furtively up and down the High Street, and, vowing me to secrecy, succumbed—but if to the visions of love's hurly-burly on tiger-skin rug or petal-strewn divan that rose and fell in the public's mind at the very sound of the authoress's name then poor Miss Baines must have felt sadly let down. Class turned out to be the film's theme, not Sex. Catherine Bush's career was social climbing; and although her sexual allure was the instrument by means of which from the reeking swamps of lower-middle philistinism she scaled the perfumed peaks of Gracious Living and Upper Classiness, it was the achievement of her ends, progressively, at each stage of her miraculous climb, that we were shown. The sexual means she had used were merely hinted at.

The fact of the matter is, however incredible it may be to those who only know the cinema in its present phase, that sex in films has not always been of paramount importance. Not at any rate before the mid 'twenties, with the establishment of Elinor Glyn as the arbiter of fashionable taste in Hollywood, the rise

Love without Words

to stardom of Clara Bow, and the production by Ernst Lubitsch of sexual comedies like *The Marriage Circle*. Until then sex was comparatively—I repeat comparatively—a minor ingredient in the stories of Hollywood films. Sex *qua* sex was strictly for blue films at stag parties or blue cinemas abroad. The importance of sex in film-making—apart from the sexual attractiveness of stars for their public—lay in the dramatic situations, the tragedies, arising from its indulgence: the misfortune of the trusting girl betrayed, the downfall of the good man gold-dug and vamped. Other than by husband and wife (off screen) the sexual act could never be performed without 'consequences'—and, babies apart, these were apt to be as dire as they were unavoidable, even when, as in *The Sign on the Door*, they took twenty years to reveal themselves. What the majority of Hollywood films were concerned with was love, not sex: love was Love, and Sex was sex, and never —or almost never—were the twain allowed to meet.

If one considers closely the films of this period and the stars who appeared in them it becomes evident that most of the characters in these movies had absolutely no use for sex at all. The fan magazine *Picture Show* used to run at this time a series of 'Expressions' of the stars: a dozen or so different close-ups of whoever the actress might happen to be (it was seldom an actor). 'Love', 'Hate', 'Jealousy', 'Remorse', one would read beneath them—sometimes with a certain amount of surprise. 'Yearning', 'Indignation', 'Suspicion', 'Nobility'—but never 'Desire', never 'Sexual Frustration', never 'Passion'—except in the sense of bad temper—and never, even to explain the most baffling, the most recondite expression, did one read 'Lust'. The simple reason was that actresses were not called upon to express such things, so many of the men who directed them having come to movies via the English or American theatre, where, in spite of Shaw and Ibsen, Victorian modes of thought were still predominant.

Can one think of a single one amongst all those female stars of the time who in her film persona did not suggest that the Victorian pundits weren't right in thinking of women as the sex without sex, of Woman as being congenitally incapable of sexual desire or of pleasure in sex fulfilment?

Take Mary Pickford for instance—the most famous and popular of them all. . . . No, definitely not Mary Pickford—whose appearances on the screen were generally in the guise of a small child, a little girl of about ten: she didn't bear much resemblance to a little girl of about ten; she looked indeed like a young woman dressed up as a little girl of about ten for a fancy-dress party. But when, forsaking this overgrown kiddywink, Mary appeared as Dorothy Vernon of Haddon Hall, moviegoers expressed their displeasure by staying away in droves. The World's Sweetheart as a young woman in her twenties, dressed and behaving like a little girl of about ten, was the World's Sweetheart as they wanted her to be.

Mabel Normand was an asexual tomboy. To mature ladies like Pauline Frederick and Clara Kimball Young sex was something they had suffered in the past for which they were being punished in the present. Lillian Gish—until she wore the Scarlet Letter in 1927—was a chaste Tennysonian dream heroine—indeed, for a brief moment amidst the rigours of *Way Down East* she appeared, a fleeting vision, as the Lily Maid of Astolat. Lillian did not, of course, any more than Mary Pickford did—to judge from Mary's baby-clasping stills of *Tess of the Storm Country* (which I never saw)—escape from having sex thrust upon her. But nobody would suggest that either of them liked the experience. As for Pearl White, she was far too busy escaping from one trap, only to fall into another, to have any time for sex. The villains may have been after her body—but with nothing more intimate in mind than to heave it overboard from a balloon or slowly lower it over a cauldron of boiling oil until she came across with the plans.

And the vamps were no better—or no worse. Nobody could have accused Theda Bara, Louise Glaum, Carmel Myers and Nita Naldi of liking sex. What Theda Bara, Louise Glaum, Carmel Myers and Nita Naldi liked was money, clothes, jewels, admiration, power over men, and ruining men's lives. Certainly these villainnesses had a great deal more *use* for sex than those heroines; but they were all sisters-in-frigidity under their skins.

Turning to the villains—we find a very odd bunch of types, some of them, it has always seemed to me, extremely suspect in their sexual villainy. In other words one didn't believe in it. They were wrongly cast. The real-life seducer, womaniser, callous conceited bastard, leaver of (pre-pill) girls in the lurch, has always and obviously been your splendid-looking, rugger-soccer-baseball-playing finest type of jolly good chap. But instead of him it was always little rodent types like Roy Darcy or Lew Cody, who suggested nothing so much as impotence. And the best actor of them all, Lowell Sherman, the most polished seducer, the most brilliant at conveying abysses of callousness, self-love and lack of heart by under-playing, in every lift of his sophisticated eyebrow, every half-shrug, blowing of smoke wreaths through pursed lips, while raising eyes to heaven, was every inch of him, in every gesture, glance, movement, every breath he took, a raving, flaming, and absolutely unmistakable queen.

And the heroes—the juveniles—of this era? Well, Douglas Fairbanks, the World's Sweetheart's husband, was so embarrassed by love scenes that he cut them to a minimum, while Wallace Reid, Charles Ray, Jack Pickford, Richard Barthelmess, Gareth Hughes and the rest of the clean-limbed golden youths had nothing more on their minds apparently than a few tender kisses followed by a march up the aisle. And the romantic lovers? Valentino naturally. At the sound of his name I see those flashing eyes, that sudden flashing of teeth as no one but he has ever flashed them. I remember a moment during *The Sheik* when the orchestra at the Putney Bridge Kinema de Luxe was playing 'Pale Hands I Loved Beside the Shalimar'—rather oddly, one might think, for a scene in the Sahara—and the conductor, inattentive to the action on the screen, missed the cue-change, so that 'Shalimar' drooled on and on in endless inappropriateness, while a desert battle raged, bullets whizzed, camels galumphed and Arabs fell.

The famous scene in this legendary film where Valentino, flinging Agnes Ayres across his saddle, gallops across the desert to the tent where he intends to have his will of her, has always been accepted as some symbol of romance—of romantic love. But here seems to be a case where Hollywood—and the public taking its cue from Hollywood—has got muddled in its use of terms. The 'romantic love' is obviously nothing but sado-masochistic libidinousness—unbridled lust—what used to be considered the sex-repressed spinster's most cherished dream. Valentino, in fact, is ludicrous in this film; everything is ludicrous: there is not a moment where sex is treated with truth or honesty; it's simply a charade. When Valentino arrives with his struggling captive in the tent, and flings her on to the divan, Agnes Ayres looks up at him and enquires like a gormless Swedish maid in an American bawdy story: 'Why have you brought me here?' It brought the house down then, and it brings the house down now.

Isn't there *any* honest, realistic treatment of sex in Hollywood films at this period? one asks oneself. Surely in Griffith's work somewhere? And there is. In the modern episode of *Intolerance* (made in 1916) there is a completely uncompromising and truthful portrayal of a working-class courtship. Robert Harron and Mae Marsh are keeping company together. Seeing her home one night after an excursion to Coney Island, the boy, madly randy, tries to force his way into her room. Mae, fighting her own urges, holds the door against him, and Harron marches off in a huff, yelling over his shoulder that he's finished with her. Mae weeps. After a moment or two Harron comes back and mutters—grudgingly at first, but then warming to the idea—Why don't they get married? And in the same film Miriam Cooper as the mistress of a gangster is quite openly and nakedly in physical thrall to him. So much so that there is one scene where the two of them embrace in such a rage of sexuality that they seem to be about to devour each other.

Valentino himself, in Rex Ingram's *The Four Horsemen of the Apocalypse*, played most movingly and delicately scenes of illicit love with Alice Terry. There is only one false note, and that comes towards the beginning of their romance, when, sitting with Miss Terry at a Tango Tea (it is during the first year of the First Great War), he murmurs: 'Come to my studio tomorrow afternoon and I promise to be good.' And he then turns straight into the camera and winks. Or as near as dammit he does.

Not a word about Von Stroheim yet, but the sexual villainy of 'The Man You'll Love to Hate', as he used to advertise himself,

Love without Words

is of course one of the cherished legends of the screen. But, as well as introducing a Krafft-Ebing type of romance into his satirical melodramas on the degeneracy of Middle European aristos, where every character, except, perhaps, the heroine, was liable, if not a sado-masochist or shoe fetishist, to be a masocho-sadistic member of the Imperial Hapsburg Monopod and Rubber Knickers Club, Von Stroheim was responsible for introducing Realistic love scenes to the silent screen. It was Realism with a capital R, in the sense that Zola had made it understood. Excrement was Truth; daffodils were lies. Nothing has ever surpassed the Realism of the first love scene between Gibson Gowland and Zasu Pitts in *Greed*. A great hulking dentist, he has raped Zasu when she was under gas. She coyly glances up at him, and then at something out of shot as they stand in the rain. 'Oh do let's go and sit on the sewer!' she suggests. Which they do, and there he asks her to be his bride.

Well, it took all kinds of Love to make the world of the dialogue-less cinema, and there was also Platonic Love, platonic not in the sense in which it has been misinterpreted, but in Plato's sense that everybody is one half of a divided whole, lost until completed again, and, until that happens, forever seeking. Nearly all the love stories in Griffith's films were based on this theory, and he was able to express it without expository titles or references to it in the dialogue by the simplest of cinematic means, which were nevertheless more telling and poignant than whole chapters of the written word—by the film language of editing. His heroines and his heroes were archetypes seldom given names: quite simply they were 'The Girl' and 'The Boy'.

In *Way Down East,* for example, Lillian Gish is trapped into a bogus marriage. Richard Barthelmess, 'The Boy', is the son of a farmer, a poet: but he and Lillian have never met, are miles apart, have no connection with each other. When Lowell Sherman as the seducer goes to put the ring on Lillian's finger it falls to the floor. Cut to Barthelmess lying on his bed, the dying sunlight falling on him through slatted blinds; suddenly he starts up in inexplicable alarm—it is as though he has heard a shot—nothing happens and he looks about him, disturbed and puzzled. Later comes the scene which to me is the most moving of all scenes of lovers' meetings, not only in the cinema but in drama and literature as well. Lillian has had her illegitimate baby, has been turned out by her puritanical landlady, and, trudging the interminable country lanes of New England, comes to the boy's farm. Hungry and exhausted, almost at the end of her tether, a slight, woebegone figure of infinite pathos, down at heel, a pale ghost in the midsummer sun, she asks for work. Barthelmess's father turns her down—a calvinist, he finds something suspicious about a young girl wandering the countryside alone. Lillian turns helplessly away. But, in the moment that she does so, the boy who is standing in the doorway of the farmhouse sees her face and recognises . . . who? what? the unknown girl's features seem as familiar to him as his own.

I have so far only spoken of Love as it was interpreted in the *American* silent cinema. The Hays Office, set up after the Virginia-Rappe-Fatty-Arbuckle scandal as a self-censorship, numbered amongst its other egregious idiocies a clause that even a married couple should not be shown in bed together unless one of them had a foot on the floor.

Films made on the Continent were not hampered in this way, but it was difficult to discern what had been originally intended in the unfolding of any story concerned with lovers because such had invariably been interfered with by the British Board of Film Censors, determined that nothing offensive to the calvinist conscience should be allowed to pollute our lilywhite screens. Titles proved invaluable when it came to hiding the true nature of what was being depicted. Garbo in *Joyless Street*, the film she made in Germany before leaving for the States to take up her Hollywood contract, as the daughter of a starving family during the post-war inflation period, sacrifices herself to obtain food for her loved ones by offering her services to the madam of a brothel. This scene, in which the ghastly depraved-looking procuress, Valeska Gert, evaluates the prospective new attraction's vital statistics to a background of unmistakable tarts in their cami-knicks, was heralded by the censor-inspired title 'Greta decides to enter a cabaret'.

In Pabst's *Love of Jeanne Ney* the lovers have been separated by the Russian revolution. She has escaped to Paris, and he, although

Love without Words

a Red, has contrived to join her. Now comes a most beautiful love scene which in 1927 left one gasping that it had been 'passed', though today it would not cause the raising of however prim-prissy an eyebrow. Wandering through the streets of Montmartre at dusk the lovers stop outside a small hotel—an hotel that seems now like a distillation of Simenon. They go in. Cut to crummy hotel room. They embrace, ecstatic with happiness. What follows may sound like sledge-hammer satire, and described in a novel it undoubtedly would be; but the fact is that on the silent screen passages like this become wonderfully transmuted. Perhaps it is because we are simply allowed to look, and to draw from what we see what conclusions we may. But I think it is for much stranger and subtler reasons.

They are together, happy, re-united, they have made love. Jeanne goes to the window and looks out. Uno comes and stands behind her, their faces 'the lineaments of gratified desire'; on their lips and in their eyes the touching, silly, reminiscent, dazzled, happy smile of two young people in the post-coital peace of passion fulfilled who are so much in love with each other that their love seems to overflow and extend to all living creatures.

What meets their gaze is a scene of violent movement behind the brightly lit window of the house across the street: a wedding party. Petite bourgeoisie are drunkenly milling; there is singing, a piano thumping, one can almost hear the crapulous bawdy jokes. Detaching herself from the party a girl comes quickly to the window, and, to conceal the fact that tears of misery are pouring down her contorted young face, pretends to be looking into the street: the bride in her starched white wedding dress with orange blossom decorations—the very picture of wretchedness, despair, terror and disgust. Egged on by his pals and newly acquired in-laws, the drunken bridegroom lurches after her. . . .

Consider the number of films turned out every year, every month, every week, every day, from studios throughout the world. With a few exceptions to prove the rule every one of these myriads of films has a love story, contains several love scenes; and the love scenes, no matter how permissive the action of the lovers, have to be expressed in dialogue; the love-scene dialogue has to be written, and we—the audience—have to listen to it. What does this dialogue consist of? What *can* it consist of—unless written by a poet—but 'I love you', 'I love you too', 'I never thought that...', 'Oh I'm so happee...', 'I love you', 'I love you too', 'Oh darling...' etc? One prays for it to stop. And one thinks, if one is old enough, with a desperate yearning and with hopeless nostalgia, of the beauty of the non-dialogue cinema, when the emotion of lovers in their scenes together was conveyed not by such trite muttered banalities but by the soaring music of Beethoven, Schubert, Tchaikowsky, Chopin, by the great musicians who have expressed what cannot be expressed in words.

Picturesque

TOURS

Autumn Night on the Dordogne
BY GEORGINA MASE

We watch the mist come creeping
   Silently up-river from the wide Atlantic,
   Sweeping round islets whose willows have known
Nothing but sun and moon and starry nights
The summer through.
Bank from bank vanishes:
Tall poplars rise from vagueness
Like moorland posts from driving snow.
Voices of man and beast,
Gurgle of water, call of bird,
Creak of oar or wheel
Come as from muffled depths, uncertain of direction,
Unreal, unattached.
Mist spreads . . . mounts . . . thickens.
The poplars disappear, and we are left
In a bewildering moon-whiteness
That shows in rifts of a cloud we feel
But cannot see.
Gone the Dordogne brightness,
The centuries-old challenge of the cliff-borne château,
The chiaroscuro of the friendly village:
We alone exist, blinded and lost,
In a nothingness of mist.

The Country of the Caves

BY HAMMOND INNES

IT WAS END-DECEMBER and there was snow on the ground as we swung under the limestone overhang and up the road that led to La Mouthe. The farm buildings were of stone, brown and old like the truffle oaks. The owner, Marie Lapeyre, was busy feeding her animals, dressed in the black habit of Périgord. When she had finished she came with an old acetylene lamp to show us her cave. We walked down a woodland path with glimpses of farmland through the trees—the dead stalks of maize still standing, the vines in neat, pruned rows, vegetable plots and grass for her cows. The truffle had not been good that year, but like most of the farmsteads of Périgord Noir it was virtually self-sufficient.

Where the trees ended, we came upon the stone ruins of the old medieval farm, and beyond was the walled-up entrance to the cave. The lamp was lit, a tiny jet of flame; a big key was inserted in the lock of the wooden door; and then we were inside, out of the cold and the snow, into a dim rock world where the air struck warm by comparison. Gourds were laid out on the floor, potatoes, and a pile of carrots showing the bleached green of new shoots. Through the centuries this had been the farm's storeroom. For a long time it had also been their *cave*, and the long gallery, with its paintings of animals engraved on the rock, was only discovered when Marie Lapeyre's grandfather ordered the *cave* to be enlarged so that he could store more of his precious wine. That was in 1895, and it was the discovery at La Mouthe that started the experts frantically searching the limestone cliff caves of the Vézère for wall paintings.

Opposite: head of a bull painted in the main hall of the Lascaux cave. Overleaf: a view of the Vézère valley, with the village of Sergeac on the right. Photograph by the author.

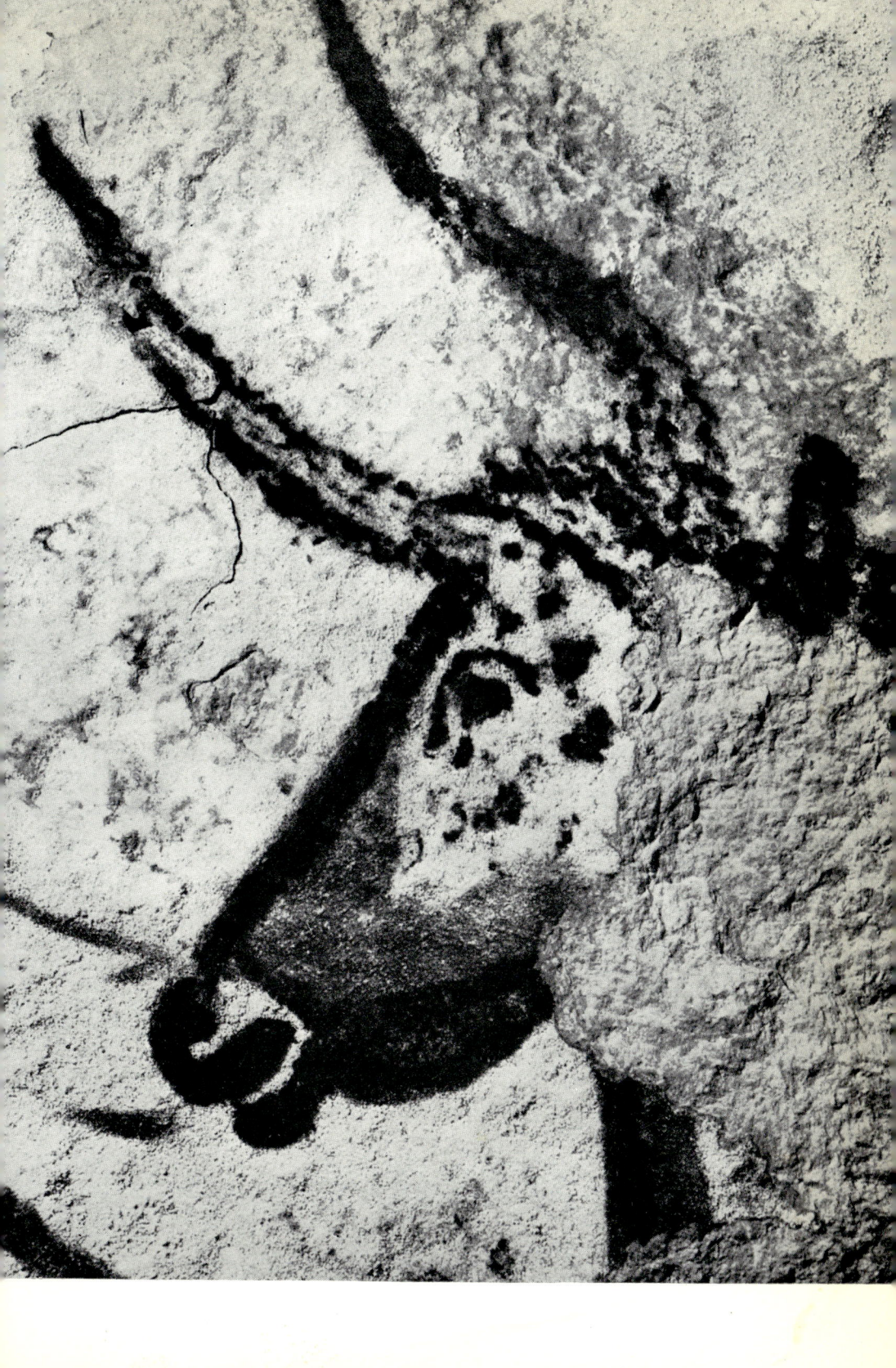

Two details from the Lascaux cave paintings. Above: an incised miniature head of a horse. Below: part of the frieze of swimming deer.

This search led ultimately to the most fabulous discovery of all—that of Lascaux in 1940. But these extraordinary and vivid paintings are relatively recent, and though we had a permit to view and were shattered by the impact, I think our favourite cave will always be the Grotte de la Mouthe. Not only because it remains the oldest of them all, the painting and engravings having been made by men who lived there sixty to eighty thousand years ago, but because of Marie Lapeyre and the very personal pride she displayed, as though she were showing us a collection of pictures in her own home.

She is a remarkable woman, a peasant landowner dedicated to a world of men so remote that we can barely comprehend their existence. As a girl she helped with the work of excavation. She was a friend of the Abbé Breuil and knew him for fifty years. She must be about sixty-five now, yet her movements were still those of a much younger woman as she flitted from wall to wall, holding the flame of her lamp to trace for us the faded shapes of horses, cattle, reindeer, bison; there was a large rhinoceros, the

A drawing by the Abbé Breuil of paintings in the Grotte de la Mouthe, showing a rhinoceros, a spotted reindeer, an ibex, a bison and three horses.

The Country of the Caves

Another drawing made by the Abbé Breuil at La Mouthe, showing an ibex superimposed on a rhinoceros, also two reindeer, a musk ox and a mammoth.

vague shape of a mammoth, and in the furthest reaches, 128 metres from the entrance, the shape of a primitive hut carved on the rock and painted in black and red.

But it was not so much the cave itself as her attitude to it that impressed us—a mixture of possessiveness and native caution. She would not tell me her name, simply saying, 'I am called Marie', and when I asked her who owned the cave she replied vaguely, 'The family'. Later I discovered that she was afraid the State might take it from her because she was not always available to show it to visitors. She was a widow, and her son, who ran the farm, was not interested. Carefully she explained to us how important it was to show the paintings by the light of a flame, since it was by lamps burning animal fat that ancient man had painted them— she still has one of the original stone lamps; the others are in the local museum. And when my wife asked, '*Est ce que vous trouviez l'ambience toujours amicable, ou quelque fois un peu affreux?*' she replied emphatically, '*Non, madame. Je le trouve émouvant que nos ancestres étaient des artistes. Très émouvant.*' Thus, simply, she expressed all her feelings, and it was with these words of hers in mind that we went on, driving through snow and winter sunshine, to explore other caves engraved and painted by the primitive hunter artists who had been our ancestors.

There are at least 1,200 caves in the area of the Dordogne and the Vézère alone. Pierre Vidal, a slender, bearded man, who is leader of the local spelaeological group and technical expert for the conservation of prehistoric remains in the area, told me that he personally had examined more than seven hundred in the past twenty years. But whilst about fifty of these could be identified as *gisements*—i.e. bearing evidence of prehistoric habitation—only about twenty, at most twenty-five, have traces of paintings or engravings. The majority of these are in the vicinity of the Vézère river, which winds back and forth between the pale grey overhanging cliffs it has cut in the limestone rock of the *causse* to join the Dordogne just below Les Eyzies. French writings often refer to this little town as the '*Capitale de la Préhistoire*'. It is an apt title, for, apart from the National Museum of Prehistory, there is a whole host of *gisements* within walking distance—Cro-Magnon, Tayac, de la Mouthe, Laugerie Haute and Basse, Abri de Poisson in the Gorge d'Enfer, Font de Gaume, which has the finest paintings outside of Lascaux, Combarelles, Les Girouteaux, with its houses built into the rock, Bernifal, Cap Blanc, and Grand Roc and Carpe Diem, two caves full of the most fantastic lime crystallisations.

Ten miles away to the north there is the Grotte de Rouffignac. It is not perhaps as important as the caves around Les Eyzies, the *gravures* having been much defaced by 'vandals' (the first in the early seventeenth century!), but as winter visitors we had this great 'Cave of the Hundred Mammoths' to ourselves, and besides the mammoths, there was something else. . . .

We drove up to it through a fairy world scintillating with the glint of sun on icicles, the brown leaves of the truffle oaks glimmering as we climbed the edge of the Forêt Barade to a big courtyarded farm. Dogs came barking and there were men repairing a roof. One of them, in gumboots and blue denims and shirt white with lime, indicated that the cave was a kilometre further on and that we should wait there. Beyond the farm we were back in the forest, and where the road ended, on the steep shoulder of a hill, we found the entrance to the cave, an iron-barred arch as big as a railway tunnel. Half an hour later the farmer I had spoken to, Monsieur Plassard, arrived on a moped, neat in brown shirt and anorak and a clean pair of trousers.

The cave was huge, and looking back, as we walked down the slope of the tunnel, I could see the warm, humid air drifting like smoke in the cold sunlight of the outside world. We came to tramlines, and, in a siding, two miniature railway trains stood waiting. In the height of the season, with a queue of tourists waiting, there would be little enchantment, but the two of us, alone with the owner, grinding slowly down into the bowels of the earth . . . it was like travelling to the ore-face in some long-deserted mine. The track was over a kilometre in length, and as the little train descended, Monsieur Plassard leaned over our shoulders, talking fast and enthusiastically, swinging his spot-light; on the ceiling first to show us the names and dates written large in the carbon black of candle flames, the work of visitors who had explored the cave long before its prehistoric significance had been appreciated. About six hundred yards in, the painting of a bison had been half obliterated, and after that we were stopping every few yards to admire the shapes of horses, goats, bison, rhinoceros, above all mammoths.

Unlike Font de Gaume and the lesser caves of the Vézère, all water-worn courses of underground rivers, Rouffignac is a sea cavern that goes back to the time when the great limestone promontories, known as '*les causses*', were reef-lines running out into the sea. Including a lower level, there are some ten kilometres of explored galleries. But ancient man only penetrated to the point where the railway ends. Here is the greatest concentration of *gravures*, mammoths chiefly, slashed with lines that are usually called 'macaroni' and which the experts believe represent the hunters' weapons. 'It is the Earth Goddess,' Monsieur Plassard explained. 'They penetrate to the greatest depth possible to be close to their god and there they make the mark of the beast they hope to kill.'

There are other marks on the wall, much deeper scratches. These are the marks of bears' claws. And there are not only their claw marks. To give visitors headroom, the line of the railway has been cut several feet below the old floor of the cavern, and for well over half the distance that floor has been pitted with huge hollows, hundreds of them. These are beds made by generations of hibernating bears, something I have never seen before. There, at the end of the line, standing in one of the pits hollowed out by a bear and surrounded by the imagined kills of our distant ancestors, we peered into the cave's continuing galleries. The next day, Monsieur Plassard told us, he would be conducting a Spanish *savant* and five students the whole length of the cave. It would be a hard day—perhaps five hours.

I would like to have joined them, but that was the day our permit allowed us to visit Lascaux. Like Rouffignac, it is on high ground—above Montignac, which is a lovely twenty-kilometre drive up the Vézère from Les Eyzies. Nothing is visible above ground, the site marked by several ugly prefabricated metal huts in a clearing amongst the pines. These are the quarters for the technicians and engineers, five of them, who have invented and maintain the complicated machinery installed to preserve the paintings. Lascaux has been closed to all but a favoured few since 1963 and we were fortunate, as foreigners, to be allowed in. Even more fortunate, we had Jacques Marsal as our guide.

Jacques Marsal was one of the four boys who discovered this extraordinary temple of prehistoric art in 1940. He was then fifteen, a keen cave explorer, and the story that they went down after their dog is pure invention—they were looking for treasure. Though the cave-hole had been used as a rubbish dump for years and had been stuffed with the branches of trees to prevent cattle from falling into it, a vague story of treasure had always been associated with it, handed down by word of mouth, possibly for centuries. What young Marsal found was a narrow chute, down which he had wriggled backwards to discover the real treasure in the light of his torch—a huge three-roomed gallery of priceless pictures.

Now you enter Lascaux through a series of airlocks and a room full of instruments. Heavy metal doors lead to a stone-vaulted ante-chamber dripping with moisture. Here you stand for a moment in a tray of liquid chemical. The next set of doors leads to the air-circulation plant, the pumps and instruments, all the home-made gadgets that record and check the work of preservation. The wall ahead is pierced by two huge air pipes, and in an aperture at floor level, a little plastic toy, like a four-board signpost, floats in a tray of water. This is the primary check, for what they have had to reproduce is the natural circulation of air, based solely on temperature, that existed before the cave was opened to the public in 1948. It was the interruption of this natural circulation, plus, of course, the breath of countless visitors, that had caused a green algae to spread rapidly over the paintings.

A further set of doors, rather like a decompression chamber, and then at last you enter the cave, and in the light of a torch the full impact of the first gallery hits you—bulls and horses, two startled bison full of the most wonderful sense of movement, the shapes getting larger as you penetrate further until a monstrous great bull sprawls across the roof. Instinctively and immediately you are comparing these paintings in your mind with the greatest treasures in the world's museums, for there is no doubt that these men, who lived and painted fifteen to twenty thousand years ago, were great artists. Their paints had an iron or manganese base, and they used them in both wet and powdered form. Their technique was to engrave the outline first and then apply their paint with a stick brush, either by strokes or dabbing; alternatively, they would blow it on as a powder. In places, the configuration of the rock has been incorporated. They could work lying on their backs; they could even retain the proportion and flow of an animal's movement when half the outline was obscured by the curve of their rock canvas.

A set of plastic doors to the right leads into a side-gallery particularly notable for its frieze of deer swimming—just the heads, yet these convey the whole impression of the struggle against the current of a swift-moving river. There is a little horse, too, that is exquisite. But it is the last and furthest gallery that makes the strongest impact. It is a vaulted tunnel of charnel-house red full of animals wounded with spears, or falling into traps. The spear lines and the trap symbols . . . suddenly you realise what this fantastic gallery is all about. This is the temple of Man the Killer. Look at that horse falling upside down. And there is another, the neck flung back in terror, the forefeet treading air as it is driven over a cliff.

It is quite likely that Lascaux will never be open to the public again. Even our visit—the entry of just three people—was recorded by instruments as a change of temperature and of air movement. This is a pessimistic view, but the authorities are very conscious of their responsibility to posterity as caretakers of the world's most unique and priceless art gallery. Only Font de Gaume has paintings of equal artistic merit, and these have already deteriorated as a result of the free flow of air since its discovery in 1901.

As we came out of the Lascaux cave, out through the doors and chambers into sunshine and fresh air, we felt a sense of unreality, as though waking from a nightmare. But deep down we knew that what we had seen is the appalling truth of our own species—the instinct of a hunter that has been handed down through 20,000 years to our own generation.

ON FOUNTAINS
BY MILES HADFIELD

PETERHOF

DRAWINGS
BY MICHAEL FELMINGHAM

Before studying this subject, we should obtain a definition. Let us take it from Johnson's *Dictionary*: 'A jet, a spout of water.' He follows it with references to Bacon and Taylor. First, Bacon:

For fountaines, they are a great beauty and refreshment ... fountaines I intend to be of two natures ... The one that sprinckleth or spouteth; the other a faire receipt of water, of some thirty or forty foot square, but without fish, or slime, or mud. For the first, the ornaments of image gilt, which are in use, do well. But the main matter is so to convey the water, as it never stay either in the bowles or in the cesterne.

Jeremy Taylor adds moral tone:

A small bason of springing water. Can man drink better from the fountain when it is finely paved with marble than when it swells over the green turf?

We are thus well informed of the three attributes of fountains. First there is the kind that throws its water high into the air, often inconsequentially; second, there is that which causes the water to tumble in a stream or splash into a large basin; and third, there is one that is more in the nature of a spring from which people drink.

In 1765 Tobias Smollett made this observation on the greatest city of fountains in the world, a city which presents an ancient and wonderful combination of great undertakings in hydraulic engineering, benificent utilitarianism, and aesthetics:

Nothing can be more agreeable to the eyes of a stranger, especially in the heats of summer, than the great number of public fountains that appear in every part of Rome, embellished with all the ornaments of sculpture, and pouring forth prodigious quantities of cool delicious water, brought in aqueducts from different lakes, rivers and sources, at a considerable distance from the city. These works are the remains of the ancient Romans, who were extremely delicate in the article of water; but, however, great applause is also due to those benificent popes who have been at the expense of restoring and repairing these noble channels of health, pleasure and convenience. This great plenty of water, nevertheless, has not induced the Romans to be cleanly ...

G

On Fountains

Montaigne, much earlier, in 1580, had observed in that always hygienically-minded country, Switzerland, that:

They have an infinite abundance of fountains in all this country; there is no village or crossroad where there are not very beautiful ones. They say there are more than three hundred in Basel by actual count.

Here it may be remarked that, presumably because of our very numerous wells, the remains of which we see in almost every village, and our singularly adequate rainfall, we British do not seem to have taken this utilitarian view of fountains until the middle of last century. On April 10, 1859, the Metropolitan Drinking Fountain and Cattle Trough Association was formed. Liverpool, it seems, had already set the example.

The desire to play with water, make it do unnatural tricks, is deeply inborn in man. Have those professors who look into our psyches ever investigated this peculiarity? As children my brothers and I had a small stream in the garden which we delighted to dam. Slowly the water would build up, and we would be fascinated by the tiny cascade that flowed over it. And then we would breach it, and be unbelievably excited by the torrent that we followed as it rushed downstream. That was nothing to the pleasure we obtained by stopping the orifice of a hose-pipe with our fingers so that the jet became highly compressed and shot higher and higher into the air. The greatest triumph, very rarely attained, was to adjust the spray in relation to the sun so that we created a rainbow. In that infantile practice lies the basic element of the whole art of fountains, developed with such combined magnificence and subtlety in Italy and France. But there is something in it which the psychiatrists should study. Somewhere, a guilt complex is involved. That this is so can be shown by the strong feelings against fountains at the time of the origins of the English landscape gardening movement. Dr Joseph Warton wrote sarcastically:

> Rich in her weeping country's spoils, Versailles
> May boast a thousand fountains, that can cast
> The tortur'd waters to the distant heav'ns . . .

Miles Hadfield

In that post-1715 microcosm of garden buildings which was Stowe no fountain found a place; Kent's Rousham got no nearer to one than his 'cold bath'—though both had cascades, which do no more than lower water from one level to another. Alexander Pope's garden had no fountain—though it must be admitted that another poet, Matthew Prior, friend of Bridgeman, who was so much concerned with the early Stowe, wrote a piece 'For the plan of a fountain on which is inscribed the effigies of the Queen on a triumphal arch, the figure of the Duke of Marlborough beneath':

> Ye active streams, where-e'er your waters flow,
> Let distant climes and furthest nations know,
> What ye from Thames and Danube have been taught
> How Anne commanded, and how Marlbro fought.

Against this, Horace Walpole, while roundly condemning Chatsworth, wrote, 'The great *jet d'eau* I like, nor would I remove it.... I except that absurdity of a cascade tumbling down marble steps, which reduces to be of no value at all.' Both, fortunately, have survived vicissitudes of taste, and we can see them today.

Having given some clues to the psychiatrists, we can return to the pleasures of fountains and their origins. We cannot do better than take as a first stage Francis Pilkington's madrigal of 1613:

> Under the tops of Helicon
>   Not far from Parnasse stately towers
> Springs forth the fountain Hippocrene
>   With banks beset with fragrant flowers.
> The hill is it my Muses use,
> The fountain which my heart doth choose.

Whether Hippocrene is the first fountain on record I do not know, but it rose from the ground in Boeotia, near Mount Helicon, when struck by the feet of the horse Pegasus, whom (it may be remembered) sprang, ready winged, from the blood of Medusa after Perseus had cut off her head. About the same time we hear of another fountain—Salmacis, in Caria near Halicarnassus, named from its presiding nymph. It was in this

On Fountains

that, at the tender age of fifteen, Hermaphroditus (son of Venus and Mercury) bathed. The result was, perhaps, unfortunate, and as my Victorian edition of Lemprière says, all males who subsequently followed his example became effeminate.

When discussing the Greeks, we should not forget their interest in matters that they found far away from their home. Herodotus, for example, recalls how in Cyrene they found the Fons Solis, which ran cool in the heat of the mid-day and warm at the rising and the setting of the sun—apparently without the aid of a nymph, or even a naiad, those 'certain inferior deities who preside over rivers, springs, wells and fountains'.

The fountains of myth, with their strange powers, only go to emphasise the importance attached to water. No human life, particularly in civilised form, can exist without it. The first fountains—really springs—used by the Greeks were enclosed to prevent fouling. The enclosures lead to decoration, and it is held that the first so treated was that of Callirrhoe, in Attica, where a lady of that name drowned herself after an unfortunate love affair. This was around 500 B.C.

Returning to the borderland of myth and history, we have Homer's description in the Odyssey of the garden of Alcinous, in which art is satisfactorily combined with utility:

> Two plenteous fountains the whole prospect crown'd;
> This through the garden leads its streams around,
> Visits each plant, and waters all the ground:
> While that in pipes beneath the palace flows,
> And thence its current on the town bestows;
> To various use their various streams they bring,
> The people one, and one supplies the King.

Moving on into history, as distinct from myth, we come to Pliny who, in about 100 A.D. wrote at such obliging length, if rather confusingly, about his villa gardens. He tells us he was not a rich man, so they may well have been typical of many others in Italy. He describes a summer house shaded by plane trees within which was a white marble alcove shading a seat from which issued jets of water as if pressed out by the weight of its occupants. This water was collected in a basin that was always filled to the brim. There was a jet throwing to a great height, and by each of the several marble seats a small fountain filled small rills that ran murmuring along, watering here and there, and refreshing the whole.

It is from Pliny's uncle, the author of the famous *Natural History*, that we learn something of another type of fountain—the simpler type which came over to Europe from Africa with the Moorish conquest of Spain. This was concerned with refreshing gardens and their paths with spray in the heat of summer. It was therefore partially concerned with irrigation. More ornamentally contrived were the single jets rising from a simple basin derived from the lotus, an indication of their ancient origin elsewhere.

As Smollett said, the greatest early water system that still is in working order—that of Rome—was begun in ancient times. To supplement the natural supply from such springs as there were, and from the River Tiber, water had to be brought from the surrounding countryside. By 226 A.D. Rome had several famous aqueducts to supply its needs, which were demanding owing to the Roman cult of the bath. It is said that there were 1,212 fountains in ancient Rome. As H. V. Morton has written in *The Waters of Rome*, 'their glory must have been one of the greatest wonders of the world. They were adorned with statues by some of the greatest sculptors of Greece and they lifted their jets or showered their cascades against the imperial background of marble temple and palace.'

Rome declined, and eventually the Goths destroyed the aqueducts. Then came the Renaissance, and those 'benificent popes who have been at the expense of restoring and repairing these noble channels of health, pleasure and convenience.' And with the health and convenience came the pleasure in a bewildering number of fountains most of which are equally consummate examples of the technique of hydraulics and of art.

Of these Italian masterpieces we are fortunate in having many descriptions written throughout the centuries. We have Montaigne's description of his visit in 1580 with four gentlemen and a guide mounted on post-horses to Castello near Florence. The house, he wrote, is of no consequence, but 'there are various things about the gardens', like the arbors of trees, such as olives and odoriferous kinds, their branches so densely interwoven that the hottest sun could not penetrate within. Then there was a big reservoir in the middle of which was a natural-looking artificial rock, which seemed all frozen over by means of the material with which the Duke (Pier Francesco de Medici) had covered his grottos at Pratolino. Above this rock was a very large bronze statue of a hoary old man seated on his rear, his arms crossed. From his beard, forehead, and hair water came steadily drop by drop, representing sweat and tears.

As the party was contemplating certain marble statues, the gardener left them. Suddenly there spurted up under their feet and between their legs jets of water from an infinite number of tiny holes, almost invisible jets of water, supremely well imitating the trickle of fine rain. The gardener, concealed some two hundred yards away, was working these jets with such artifice that they would rise and fall, or turn and move their direction just as he wished.

They then saw the master fountain, which issued from a conduit in two very big bronze effigies, of which the lower half (Hercules), holding the other (Antaeus) in his arms, appeared to squeeze him with all his might, so that he fainted. With his head thrown back, Antaeus seemed 'to spurt this water forcibly out of his mouth; and it shoots out with such power that the stream of water rises thirty-seven fathoms above the height of these figures, which were at least twenty feet high'.

Last came the grotto, with all sorts of lifelike animals spouting water from beak, wing, claw, ear or nostril.

Montaigne does not here mention another admired feature of Renaissance fountains—those that produced, as a sideline, loud explosions.

France was to carry on the art and craft of garden design as the Renaissance impetus declined in Italy and moved northwards. The period of its greatest glory was during the reign of Louis XIV and under the dominating influence of Le Nôtre. By this time *le jardin français* had developed a distinct character of its own. As one student has pointed out, the French classic style had evolved within its own country; it was neither imposed upon France nor a sudden invention. It was much more logical, and the fountains, superbly designed and wrought though they were, played their part in an over-all design—they were not isolated, star performers, as inevitably were many of the finest fountains of Italy. The whole attitude towards gardens was different from that in Italy: 'the nation and the court wished to be dazzled and enchanted by novelty and singularity'—well displayed in the mechanical elaboration and brilliance of the fountains. Le Nôtre's gardens, too, mostly lay in open, level country. In 1712 the savant d'Argenville wrote:

> Fountains next to plants are the principal ornaments of gardens: 'tis these that seem to animate them, by the murmuring and spouting of their waters, and produce those admirable beauties, that the eye is scarce ever satisfied with beholding them. They are constantly set in the most advantageous places, and where they may be best seen from all parts. If there be any sloping ground in the garden, you may then make cascades and buffets of water, continued by several falls, accompanied with spouts and *jets d'eaux;* and, where water is plenty, ponds and canals may be made, which are most delightful pieces in a garden. Upon these canals, you may have small gilt gondolas and pleasure-boats, and they should be very well stocked with fish, for the diversion of fishing in them. To add still farther to the ornament of the water, swans, geese and ducks of different kinds and colours, are a very agreeable sight.

The major *jet d'eau* was placed as the culminating point of a main walk or vista passing through groves, either on its own and surrounded by bosquets, or in the grandest manner, 'beyond the groves is a large canal, reaching the whole breadth of the garden; in the midst of which is a group of figures, as Neptune and Tritons, throwing one great spout, and many lesser every way'.

A great deal of attention is given to the construction and management of fountains. As a contrast to the aqueducts and power of gravity so usual in Italy, we gather that generally 'the natural water not to be found in a flat and dry country, you must have recourse to water-engines, which raise it from the bottom of wells, into receiving cisterns and high places for the purpose of carrying it afterwards into the gardens'.

These local supplies raised by the engines are, we learn,

On Fountains

generally preferred to bringing water along an aqueduct from a distance: for one thing, 'they bring the spring into the house, which spares the continual grief of seeing the conduit-pipes broke by the malice of country fellows, that take delight in anything that will mortify a gentleman.'

We can gain the best impression of these great fountain courtyards from eighteenth-century engravings. Always the scene is crowded with people posturing, sitting, being wheeled in chairs, parading, talking, laughing—all those persons familiar to us from the works of the eighteenth-century figure painters.

So complex and stupendous was the fountain system at Versailles that a writer early in the last century assures us that it played in its entirety only on one day in the year and then at its fullest extent for half an hour, which cost £3,000.

The Renaissance jokers do not seem to have played a part in the fountains and waterworks of the Sun King. And the designers who worked for Le Nôtre, superb craftsmen though they were, had not quite the genius of the masters of the Renaissance.

Yet Le Nôtre's style of gardening, and even French garden architects associated with it, dominated much of the world in spite of the international spread of *le jardin anglais*. Le Blond and his successor worked for Peter the Great at Peterhof, which has one hundred and twenty-six fountains and three cascades. Robillon carried the style to Queluz in Portugal, while Drottningholm in Sweden is a further example of 'gallomania'.

While the great Renaissance fountains of Rome were being built, it seems that the best England could do was to elaborate the conduits from which utilitarian water was obtained. By Tudor times something better was being done. In about 1529 Skelton wrote:

> In the midst of a conduit, that curiously was cast,
> With pipes of gold, engushing out streams;
> Of crystal the clearness these waters far past,
> Enswimming with roaches, barbellis and breams,
> Whose scales ensilvered against the sunbeams,
> Englistered, that joyous it was to behold . . .

Later in the century the Lumley Inventory gives descriptions and drawings of 'marble lavabos, cisterns and fountains'. Yet there is no fountain at the centre of the garden shown on the title page of Gerard's *Herball* of 1597, though by 1618 William Lawson shows quite an elaborate conduit as a central feature.

These were gentleman's or yeoman's gardens.

Royal gardens, however, were doing better. Travellers from the Continent who visited England in 1598 and 1599 described how at Hampton Court 'there are two fountains that spout water one round the other like a pyramid, upon which are perched small birds that stream water out of their bills. In the grove of Diana is a very agreeable fountain, with Actaeon turned into a stag, as he was sprinkled by the goddess and her nymphs. . . . There is besides another pyramid of marble full of concealed pipes, which spurt upon all who come within their reach.' The Renaissance joker had reached England!

At Nonsuch there was a very handsome and elaborate snow-white fountain, showing a griffin angrily spewing water with great violence. At Windsor there were several fountains, including one artistically wrought of lead, while another of white marble was being erected, with £70 sterling already spent on it and a channel that conducted the water from four miles away. The new Tudor aristocracy was also making fountains. At Burleigh's Theobalds in 1598 he had a *jet d'eau* with a basin of white marble. From the next reign came Bacon's instructions on this subject, while an elaborate fountain base of about 1615 designed by John Smythson at Bolsover Castle can still be seen.

It is pleasant to turn back from this splendour—far though it was from that attained on the Continent—to an idyllic and mythical place recalling our own days of myth. It was described by Fynes Moryson when he was at Warwick in 1617:

> Not far thence is a transparent and pleasant, but little wood, and there by clear fountains, which place yields sweet solitude for the Muses, and there they report, that the famous worthy Guy of Warwick after many adventures achieved, did first live an heremites life, and was after death buried.

It is an abrupt change to the grandeur of Wilton, where the first garden (of which traces still remain) was designed by Isaac

On Fountains 118

de Caux in 1632. Fortunately, the fountains were still in working order when Celia Fiennes made a visit in about 1685:

> The grottoe... is garnished with many fine figures of the Goddesses, and about two yards off the door is several pipes in a line that with a sluice spouts water up to wet the strangers, in the middle room is a round table, a large pipe in the midst, on which they put a crown or gun or a branch, and so it spouts the water through the carvings and points all round the room at the artist's pleasure to wet the company; there are figures at each corner of the room that can weep water on the beholders... and also it is so contrived in one room that it makes the melody of nightingales and all sorts of birds which engaged the curiosity of the strangers to go in to see.

Even more extraordinary was the display of hydraulics in the garden of Thomas Bushell, once page to Bacon, later a speculator and mining engineer, which was visited by Charles I and Queen Henrietta in 1636. It was at Neat Enstone, not far from Blenheim, and was supplied by the same little River Glyme that feeds 'Capability' Brown's lake. We have an excellent eyewitness account written in 1635:

> On the side of a hill is a rock some 11 or 12 feet from the bottom whereof (by turning of a cock) rises and spouts up about 9 feet high a stream which raiseth on his top a silver ball, and as the said stream riseth or falleth to any pitch or distance, so doth the ball, with playing, tossing, and keeping continually at the top of the said ascending stream: the which after it gains the top, descends not again into that current, but runs into the rock and there disperseth itself.

There was the usual joke, a hedge of water, crossing like a plashed fence, 'whereby sometimes fair ladies cannot make the crossing, flashing and dashing their smooth, soft and tender thighs and knees, by a sudden enclosing of them in it'. More original was a chamber from which descended artificial showers under which a man might stand, quite dry, in the sunshine, surrounded by rainbows.

After the Restoration Evelyn wrote of the new 'rich and noble fountain, with sirens, statues, etc. cast in copper by Fanelli', but unfortunately with 'no plenty of water', at Hampton Court (it is the Diana fountain, now included within Bushey Park). In his *Kalendarium Hortense* for December he gives a warning to the English fountain-owner of some significance: 'Look to your fountain pipes, and cover them with fresh and warm litter out of the stable, a good thickness, lest the frosts crack them; remember it in time, and the advice will save you both trouble and charge.'

Our climate surely plays some part in our failure to become great fountaineers. Foreigners, from de Caus onwards, have been concerned with them: the most famous fountain at Blenheim, for example, is the work of Bernini, and was given to the Duke

The Emperor fountain, Chatsworth

On Fountains

of Marlborough in 1710. And if the illustrations of 'All Sorts of Fountains' in John Worlidge's *Systema Horticulturae, or the Art of Gardening* of 1677 is anything to go by, our standard of design was low. His surprise fountain has a jet shooting from the breast of, presumably, Venus into the eye of a gentleman's lady love.

In the next century, as we have already seen, our fountains ceased to play. In a work which was the amateur's handbook, and which dealt with, for example, the design of garden houses, Isaac Ware's *Complete Body of Architecture*, fountains are not mentioned. And the international spread of the vogue for *le jardin anglais* to some extent discouraged fountains elsewhere.

However, the early nineteenth century saw a great revival. Loudon in his *Gardener's Magazine* from 1826 described many patterns, particularly those made in artificial stone. Never of outstanding grandeur, and usually including dolphins in their design, they accorded well with the taste of the rising class of wealthy businessmen and industrialists who were building the new suburban villas and country houses.

In this century, too, were built England's two most famous fountains. The first was the Emperor fountain at Chatsworth, designed by Paxton for a visit of the Emperor of Russia which never materialised. It takes its water from the hills above, and is a fine piece of hydraulic engineering. It is an exciting experience to watch its custodian turning it on with a large key. This operation, and even more turning it off, needs the greatest care, because an immense pressure of water is built up in the pipe, 'as large as sewer', that feeds it. The jet slowly rises up to spray the tops of the surrounding lime trees. When the wind blows towards the house it cannot be turned to full strength as the spray drifts to the building, soaring over the jets of the seventeenth-century fountain which Walpole approved. The water at full pressure reaches 276 feet. Chatsworth, indeed, is a fountain-lover's paradise, for there also are jets that roar around Archer's temple which originate the cascade, and a willow tree of copper whose branches shower water.

England's other great fountain is in the garden of Witley Court in Worcestershire, though it is now dry, and as derelict as the rest of that once famous garden, which was more or less com-

Nesfield's great fountain at Witley Court, Worcestershire

pleted in the 1860s (it was never quite finished). The designer of the fountain, showing Perseus striking at the dragon to rescue Andromeda, was the retired soldier W. A. Nesfield, and the sculptor the local mason James Forsyth. It was one of the largest groups of statuary in Europe. It weighed 20 tons and rose 24 feet from the waterline. A steam engine threw the main jet into the air. It formed 'dissolving views of shifting rainbows, and with the rush, dash, splash and light feathery spray of the many rising and falling streams or jets one seems riveted to the spot, as by the spell of all the water-nymphs' enchantments. The flowers even seem to lose their brilliance.' It cost over £20,000.

Nesfield's Witley Court fountain shows a revolution in the mechanics of hydraulics: the 40 h.p. steam engine throwing the main jet to 120 feet. No longer was the elemental force of gravity

On Fountains 122

needed, no longer was the height of the jet limited by the level of the cistern which fed it. Yet it cannot be said that during the nineteenth century any great imagination was shown in the design of fountains. The old classical forms were repeated with no great distinction and little imagination in the handling and trickery of the jets themselves.

The revival of medieval styles then affected the fountain; strange structures in an ecclesiastical manner were erected, cold

Victorian fountain at Denman College

and unexciting compared with the great works of ancient time. Such a one stands in Birmingham—a solitary, isolated representative of the ancient art of fountain-making in one of England's greatest cities. It splashes clumsily into a basin, and in so doing appropriately commemorates that solid statesman Joseph Chamberlain: the small area in which it stands is known locally and ignominiously as 'Squirt Square'. It is, of course, supplied by the efficient municipal supply of water brought—a fine achievement of hydraulic engineering—from the romantic valleys of Wales. Still, on hot days, the children enjoy paddling in the basin, unaware that it has in its ancient lineage the city fountains of Rome, and of Paris, and quite unconscious (as surveyed by a policeman) of the great fun that the Renaissance jokers would have provided for them. And what would the citizens have thought of the nymphs at Schönbrunn?

Water in abundance returned in the present century. Though not alone in the revival, the outstanding designer was the Swede, Carl Milles. His figures of gods, humans and monsters of the deep, life-like yet executed in a distinctly personal stylised manner, have an almost baroque feeling of movement, and the jets and sprays are thrown about freely and with abandon. His work, always on a magnificent scale, is to be seen not only in Sweden but in the United States. The period saw, too, a number of delightful fountains with rather stylised and simplified human and animal figures. One good example is in Hyde Park: a dancing couple, by T. B. Huxley Jones. None of these has the flamboyance of Milles, who may well be the last master of the grand, humane fountain.

For, as in other art forms during the last few decades, the human being known and imagined since the days of Adam and Eve has disappeared. Instead we have many ingenious devices, to which are attached various names, which are principally concerned with the relations of inhuman forms and objects one to another, frequently in space. Whether this is perpetually satisfying to the deeper, more searching aspects of man's psyche is dubious. Yet surely, this kind of art—not infrequently concerned with motion—is particularly suitable for the creation of objects concerned with the impermanence of moving water, though this may sometimes be contrasted with the intense calm of water that is static. Fountains of this type have been produced, making use both of our increased scientific knowledge of the behaviour of liquids in motion, and of the many new materials that may be used in contrivances to control these movements.

Some fountains already are concerned with no more than the behaviour of water, the structures being little more than a frame enabling this to be effected. An example was seen at a horticultural show at Stuttgart, which, from photographs, appears to have been singularly effective.

What, we may ask after this brief discussion of fountains, is the appeal that they have for us, beyond the simple fascination of the child watching something that appears, at an early age, to be 'against nature'? Perhaps it is the even more elemental one, vitally important in a hot country, of providing cool water to quench thirst and for ablutions, not only physical but symbolic and mystical. Perhaps we should, when summarising the spiritual attributes of fountains, recall Augustus Montague Toplady's most glorious hymn:

> Nothing in my hand I bring,
> Simply to thy Cross I cling;
> Naked, come to thee for dress;
> Helpless, look to thee for grace;
> Foul, I to the Fountain fly;
> Wash me, Saviour, or I die.

At the other extreme there is the boastful impulse which causes man to demonstrate his domination over the most intractable of elements, converting it by his own skill from a state of flatness and immobility in a calm pond to one of violent agitation with almost aeriform qualities.

The fountain has other attractions, not least of which is its effect on light: it enables man, when the sun shines, to create God's bow, making the covenant that showed to Noah that there would be no other flood. And at night we can illuminate the spray artificially to produce a new, mysterious beauty.

And, particularly at night, there is sound: did not Respighi attempt to perpetuate this when they are silent—as they will all one day, become—in his *Fontane di Roma*?

Orpheus fountain by Carl Milles, Cranbrook Academy, Michigan

Romantic America
PAINTINGS BY
Felix Kelly
COMMENTARY
BY ROBERT HARLING

THANKS TO the early influences of Brighton, I have long had a passion for architecture, preferably domestic. The dolls' house façades of those small flint houses; the majestic monotony of those great squares and crescents; the beguiling Hindoo nonsense of the Royal Pavilion, seen first as a schoolboy, have remained major visual pleasures ever since.

To one so architecturally obsessed, Felix Kelly's first one-man show in London during the war inevitably proved a very heady experience.

He was in the RAF, but had managed to stage a show at Reid & Lefevre's Gallery in King Street, St James's. I was on leave, looked in at the gallery on a solitary saunter, took one look at the paintings, knew that this was the way I also saw houses (and would have liked to have painted them) and wanted to buy the lot.

On naval pay I bought one, a small painting of a pepper-pot stuccoed Regency house fallen on evil days, with a dog-cart, also down on its uppers, as part of the *mise-en-scène*. I took the painting back to sea. I still have it; now, happily, along with others, larger.

I also experienced on that occasion a first pang of bitter-sweet pleasure which has always for me been inseparable from enjoyment of Kelly's paintings, whether seen privately or in a gallery. The experience is neither enviable nor laudable: it is just that I invariably want to own both the paintings *and* the houses.

This is due partly to the fact that Kelly paints only houses he likes, but mainly because he is a rare master of the art of evoking the *mood* of a house. The misty grandeur which attends a Stately Home set remotely and preposterously on some moorland eminence; the gaiety of an old rectory now inhabited by the carefree children of pagan parents; the melancholy of a great Palladian mansion set in the misty keys of the Deep South; the mystery encompassing a Georgian manor house now little more than a granary for some Lincolnshire farmer . . . such houses of mood are recorded by Kelly in much the same way that Hilliard, with insight yet detachment, could record the baleful arrogance of a warrior or the soulful languor of a poet—and there is much of a miniaturist's technique in Kelly's work.

Apart from an unceasing list of commissions in this country and in the United States, Kelly is always seeking out these houses of mood. He is incurably curious about houses and a widely read student of domestic architecture. When he is not painting he is likely to be driving fast yet observantly in his TR4A towards some house of which he has heard report in a distant corner of Britain. Such houses, too often neglected by owners and artists alike (for artists, in common with so many contemporary architects, seem increasingly disinterested in houses of yesteryear), are the mainspring of Kelly's life.

For some, Kelly is a romantic, but—like realist—this is a label that defies exact definition. Weren't Elizabethans the most rugged realists in our history and yet the most extravagantly romantic?

We are, we are always being told, living in an age (perhaps The Age) of Realism. Everybody has to be a realist, whether he or she likes it or not. But there are, of course, snags. The first and toughest is that the realist and the romantic are apt to be co-existent in each of us in variable immeasurable degrees. The other is that one man's realism is another man's escapism.

Those who live in houses painted by Kelly need suffer from no such dichotomies. His work resolves, for them, the most extreme of polarities, being possessed of all the necessary data of realism—an exactitude of glazing-bars, a certainty of brickwork and so on—yet capturing the exact *mood* of their houses.

I well remember that old realist Lord Kemsley (who sold out

Romantic America

to Roy Thomson the great Sunday newspaper he had built up and claimed he loved above all things) being knocked for six by a pair of paintings of his house that he had commissioned from Kelly. He was surprised by the fact that he couldn't fault the paintings as depictions of the home of which he was so proud, but he was strangely moved by the way that Kelly had, as he said, 'caught the atmosphere of the house', which, indeed, he had—and there are few more romantic-looking houses in southern England than Dropmore in Buckinghamshire, its architectural history somewhat hazy but certainly touched by Wyatt.

Some indication of the unusual response of those who are hooked by Kelly's skills is shown by the requests he frequently receives for paintings. 'What of?' he asks, preparing to take to his car to inspect the house, at least. Not a bit of it. Some of his would-be patrons don't live in that kind of house. They just love his paintings and just want him to provide them with one of his *capricci* so that they can contemplate at their leisure a forsaken house in its lakeside setting, a Batty Langley gothick folly atop a Shropshire knoll, a splendid stuccoed museum in an exotic landscape . . . when they are in that kind of mood.

The fact is that Kelly, like any true portraitist, captures the many elements which make up any unusual, beautiful, interesting, memorable, handsome façade, and people respond to the portraits.

Like those Elizabethans he is at once realist and romantic.

The paintings by Felix Kelly that follow are reproduced by courtesy of Messrs Arthur Tooth & Sons.

OLD RAILROAD CAR
CHAPMAN, ALABAMA
1967

THE HOUSE and the car exist, and both belong to Mr Earl M. McGowin, a director of the Louisville and Nashville Railroad. As an outstanding businessman and with a predilection for the notable engines that opened up the United States, Mr McGowin rescued this magnificent car and locomotive, complete with its funnel-shaped stack. There is one element of the *capriccio* in the painting: house and car are rather more distant from each other than the painting would have one believe.

130

THIS IS a complete and thoroughly wilful *capriccio*. The house is a composite rendering of a Deep South mansion, composed of most of the neo-classical architectural elements that give these houses their romantic poignancy, and which the artist admits he is ready to respond to wholeheartedly. The miniature railway is an added whim. Such railways would be favoured toys of the artist if he lived in such state and on such an estate. 'So why not indulge my pleasure on canvas?' he asks, and thereupon does just that.

MINIATURE RAILWAY
NEW ORLEANS
1967

TWIN HOUSES
MISSISSIPPI
1968

UNLESS he has been commissioned by a patron to depict that patron's house *in situ*, so to speak, Kelly is apt to move his houses around the way chess-players move pawns around. Thus the fine twin houses seen in this painting were first seen by the artist in the French Quarter of New Orleans, but he saw them as more evocative and appropriate to a *bayou* off the great Mississippi, and, with the licence most artists give themselves in such circumstances, forthwith translated them a hundred miles away.

FERRY
MARTHA'S VINEYARD
1968

T HIS PAINTING could almost be termed a documentary *capriccio* or *vice versa*, for all the elements exist—disparately. The ferry exists, the pier exists and the reeds exist, but the composition is the artist's own particular pleasure. 'One sees these scenes of romantic dereliction in one's wanderings along the New England coast. They remind me, too, of odd corners of New Zealand seen as a boy. So it's almost second nature to paint them. This study is one of many.'

133 Not so far south this time. This painting is really a reconstruction of two reconstructions. The 'Charles W. Morgan' is a reconstruction of a nineteenth-century whaling ship, and, after the restoration, the craft was berthed in the port of Mystic, Connecticut, which itself is to be a reconstruction of a typical whaling town, so well depicted in the novels of Melville, Hergesheimer and others. Kelly, impatient for these projects to be completed, placed the whaling ship in an imagined quayside setting, complete with lighthouse, one of the recurrent motifs in his nautical paintings.

THE CHARLES W. MORGAN
CONNECTICUT
1968

IN MUCH the same manner that the streetcars of New Orleans have captured the imagination of Tennessee Williams, they have consistently fired Kelly's imagination. 'This is no particular corner of New Orleans,' says the artist, 'but visitors to that city will recognise it as typical of scores of corners they remember. For myself, I made dozens of sketchbook notes of these streetcars and, inevitably, scores of notes of the cast-iron canopies and balconies which are so individual a fantasy feature of the city. Here I combined them in what I suppose one could call a *capriccio* recollected in tranquillity.'

STREETCAR
NEW ORLEANS
1968

VETERAN AND VINTAGE
ROSEMOUNT, ALABAMA
1968

ANOTHER Kelly *capriccio* based on scattered items of fact and fancy. The derelict house seen here is the mansion known as Rosemount. The artist saw the house on one of his many travels through the states of the Deep South and, taken by the magnificently emphatic mirador, with look-out room, atop the porticoed main structure, made sketches. Veteran cars are his particular passion, as they are increasingly of many well-heeled Americans. 'So I put in three of my own favourites,' says the artist, 'and let the composition make its own story for anyone who sees the painting.'

Romantic America

OPPOSITE are shown two more examples of Kelly's studies in romantic melancholy and eerie fantasy, with both paintings demonstrating delight in historic locomotives, whether full-scale or miniature models. Is there a story attached to either painting? 'Only the stories you make up yourself when you see the paintings,' Kelly says. For himself there are no stories.

Above:
THE MINIATURE RAILWAY ENTHUSIAST, 1967
Below:
OLD LUMBER LOCOMOTIVE, CHAPMAN, ALABAMA, 1966

A MISH-MASH OF THE ARTS

A Date with a Dame
BY FRED BASON

FLORA ROBSON made her first appearance on any stage at Enfield in 1908, when she was five. It was at a school concert where she recited 'Little Orphan Annie' (with actions). As an encore she recited two other pieces that she had learnt before she was six years old—and with actions as well. I was not present at this memorable performance because I was one year old at the time.

She began her professional career in 1921. It was at the Shaftesbury Theatre, in Clemence Dane's *Will Shakespeare*. The play was produced by Basil Dean and the cast included Mary Clare and Philip Merivale. It is probable that I saw this play because Mary Clare was the first famous actress I was friendly with. I had seen Mary Clare in a play called *The Return of the Soldier*, which had the notices up to close at the end of the week. With the cockney impudence I had in my 'teens I sat down and wrote to fifty important people, appealing to them to support this sad but brilliant play. The play ran for many weeks instead of a few days!

But, to return to Flora Robson, I have no recollection of seeing her in *Will Shakespeare*, but as she appeared as a ghost I have an alibi. I remember very well, though, when she *did* come into my life. It was in 1932, when she appeared in a play by Somerset Maugham called *For Services Rendered*.

Maugham had given me a front-row seat in the grand circle for the first night. I sat next to his Swiss valet. I made a joke or two, but the valet never smiled. Nor did either of us smile during *For Services Rendered*. It was a very sad play.

The first-night audience was not in sympathy with this sad play. There was coughing and a murmur of voices. Someone in the gallery called 'Speak up, please!' with some justification.

Flora was cast in the role of a spinster, aged around forty. She had to propose marriage to a retired Navy man who was desperately trying to make a living in civilian life and failing to do so. His embarrassing rejection of her proposal led to a bout of hysterics, and she was carried off the stage screaming. Her

A Date with a Dame

screams could be heard in the wings. Maugham's valet exclaimed: 'What sadness!' I didn't answer. I couldn't. I was weeping.

At the fall of the curtain Flora got an ovation. I stood up and cheered. 'Bravo, Flora! Bravo, Flora!' I called out. I knew that from that day onwards I would be her admirer for the rest of my life. Maugham's valet stared at me in astonishment as he clapped politely. The lady on my right, however, had been weeping for the past quarter of an hour, and was still weeping as I stood up shouting 'Bravo!'

Afterwards the valet asked me to have dinner with him, but I declined as the suit I was wearing was frayed at the cuffs and I was wearing the navvy's boots that I had to wear when I was selling books off my barrow in the street. But I went back-stage to thank Maugham for sending me a ticket. I couldn't find him; but I got Flora's autograph. She said 'Thank you for asking me!' and there were tears in her eyes. I remember that I had to climb three flights of stairs to get to her dressing room, and there were only three people there whilst there must have been thirty in Cedric Hardwicke's dressing room.

Three times I saw this play during its short run of six weeks, and each time Flora's acting caught at my throat and I was moved to tears. To me it was not just acting; she seemed to be breaking her heart. I was afraid that the sustained hysteria might do her some physical harm. In fact I was really rather glad when the play ended and she no longer had to break her heart—and mine—every night. The fact is I had fallen in love with her.

The next play I saw Flora in was an all-out flop called *Head-on Crash*. Dame Flora will remember this play because it was probably the worst in which she has ever appeared and the first in which her name was up in lights—and she was given star billing. The gallery booed this senseless, almost incomprehensible play. I did *not* boo. I sent her a bunch of eight roses. Why eight roses? Because I lived for years at number 152—add these numbers together and you get eight. I paid eight shillings for the bunch, which was a great deal of money to me in those far-off days. I did not put my name on the label. I simply put 'With fond regards from an admirer'. The play was off in about three weeks.

Flora's next appearance was with Paul Robeson in Eugene

O'Neill's *All God's Chillun got Wings*. I saw it at the Piccadilly Theatre in about the third week of its run. I had been seriously ill, having caught a severe chill at my barrow, which turned to pneumonia. Whilst the press raved over the great acting of Flora I was fighting to stay alive. I pulled myself together the best way I could, and a friend took me in his car to see the *tour de force* of Flora's brilliant performance in this play. As Ella she got her first real chance and she took it with both hands.

The other star of this play was Paul Robeson, and I said to him one day: 'If I had a hat I'd raise it to you in admiration, but all I can do is raise my cap.' He laughed at this and said: 'I often wear a cap. I must send you a photograph of myself wearing one.' And he did! I like to think he had it taken specially for me, but perhaps I'm kiddin' myself. The odd thing is that when I show people this photograph and say: 'There's Paul Robeson wearing a cap,' nobody seems to think it odd. But can *you* imagine Paul Robeson wearing a cap? I can't; and I certainly never saw him wearing anything on his head at all. Paul Robeson in a cap!

After seeing Eugene O'Neill's play I had to leave off going to first nights for a long time. I had neither the money nor the time to spare. I had acquired a bookshop. True it was only a small bookshop—being less than seven feet wide. It was in New Church Road, Camberwell. I had no competition; but also I had no customers! No money to spare for theatre-going!

Meanwhile I knew that Flora was making an even greater name for herself at the Old Vic and elsewhere. Acting with Charles Laughton and my loyal friend of the past forty years, Marius Goring, must have been a help to her. Perhaps the most important part she played at this time was that of Gwendolen Fairfax in *The Importance of Being Earnest*, because it proved to all the world that she could excel in parts that were *not* unhappy.

I didn't see her in *Mary Tudor*, which I believe followed her season at the Old Vic, because then I was travelling over Europe and even to some parts of Africa gathering together sets and specimens of cigarette cards. Yes, cigarette cards! I had landed myself a really lovely job writing a weekly article on cigarette cards for *Tit Bits* which lasted right up to the day the Second World War started. I came back from Hamburg on the last boat

A Date with a Dame

out of that city with a suitcase full of German cigarette cards.

I only once heard about Flora during the war, when a dear friend of mine, Beatrice Winkler, went to see her at the Henry Miller Theatre in New York City in a play called *Ladies in Retirement*. She had nothing but praise to write to me. I sent Flora a postcard on which I wrote: 'Please *don't* retire! We can't spare you! Your London Admirer Fred.' Of course she knew nothing about it, but I was still in love with her.

Now we come to a more personal part of the story. Around my sixty-first birthday I had a load of trouble that I could hardly bear. In a wave of depression I took all the sleeping pills I had—about a dozen. I didn't die, but I had an agonising heart attack. The sweat poured off me with sheer pain. I managed to open my door and slide down the stairs into the street, where I was picked up by two policemen at two o'clock in the morning and taken back to my bedroom. One of them made me black coffee and the other walked me up and down the room. Perhaps they thought I was drunk! Anyway, I was very sick; and then I went to sleep.

It was light when I woke up. I was in less pain. One of the policemen was still with me. Seeing him I burst into tears. Then I went to sleep again. When I woke again he had gone. They never came back, but I shall never forget their kindness.

After this I felt a terrific need for company, to get out and mix with people and get a grip on life again. I wrote to a famous comedian with whom I was acquainted and asked if I could come and have a chat with him. I thought he'd cheer me up. I enclosed a stamped and addressed envelope for his reply; but one never came. Then I sat down and wrote to Flora Robson, knowing she had read my writings in *The Saturday Book*, and asking if I could come and see her. I didn't enclose a stamp this time.

She replied by return of post, inviting me to tea with her at six o'clock at the Haymarket Theatre, where she was appearing in a revival of *The Importance of Being Earnest*. As I waited for her to arrive, at the stage door, wearing a brand-new cap which I had bought for the occasion, a pigeon up above gave me a warm, wet welcome. (The cornice above the stage door at the Haymarket Theatre is a great hang-out for pigeons.)

I was a bit annoyed that my new cap was messed up, but I remembered that it's supposed to be lucky when this happens to anyone. And so it was. When Dame Flora arrived she had brought two big sugary doughnuts from Brighton, specially for me. I drank tea with her. We talked and talked, and as I've been stage-struck all my life I found I knew many of the people she knew. Thirty minutes flashed by. Then I knew she had to change and make-up for the evening performance.

I kissed her hand, but she—dear wonderful lady—held me to her and gave me a real kiss. Then she asked me to come again the following Friday.

I did, and again we talked and talked. She said she'd like to retire at the end of the run of the Oscar Wilde revival. She said she had worked very hard for more than forty-five years; that she had never really explored her beloved Sussex, and she felt she deserved a rest. I agreed with her. After all, her dressing room (nice as it was) was on the third floor, and heaven knows how many times she had to climb those stairs during a year's run.

But on the very next visit to her I learnt that she was engaged to appear in Anouilh's *Ring Round the Moon*. I said 'What about your retirement plans?' She shrugged her shoulders and said she could not afford to turn down work—but she had decided to give it till 1971, when she would have been fifty years on the stage. I suggested that because of the much discussed rigging of art sales that magnificent play by Emlyn Williams, *The Late Christopher Bean*, would be a very good play in which to appear for her farewell performance. She pointed out that Dame Edith Evans had created the part of the Welsh housekeeper and that she (Flora) could never hope to carry the conviction of someone Welsh. 'After all, dear, Edith is Welsh! I come from South Shields.' But within ten seconds she was speaking with such a very Welsh accent that, shutting my eyes, I was listening to a very, very Welsh lady. The truth is that Dame Flora Robson is the most *modest* distinguished actress I have ever known.

At the end of our third tea party she asked if I would care to spend a day with her at Brighton. She would meet me in her car and we would go for a drive around Sussex. Would I? Would I! We met at ten at Brighton Station and she drove me back to the

A Date with a Dame

station at seven that evening. Flora gave me one of the happiest days of all my sixty-two years of living.

I was drinking a Pimms Number One by about eleven. We had chicken for luncheon. We had tea under an old apple tree at Alfriston, where she bought me an expensive, beautifully made tea-pot stand with a map of Sussex in the centre of it. She also bought me a large jar of local honey 'to fatten you up'.

We had a couple of glasses of sherry when we arrived back at Flora's home. I was given a packet of cigarettes, a large lump of cake and some French pastries to take home. It was five to seven when we reached Brighton Station. I was too full of sherry and emotion to say a proper 'Thank You'.

I went down to see her again in October, and on this occasion she gave me proof of her magnificent memory by reciting to me (with actions) 'Little Orphan Annie', as she had recited it at the school concert at Enfield when she was five. She also gave me a lesson in elocution, showing me how to overcome echoes in large halls by using clipped words instead of rounded phrases. We talked and she knitted, and then we returned to London in a first-class carriage all to ourselves.

She gave me back so much self-confidence that I went to the Isle of Man next day and gave two very merry lectures to the Manx. And she gave me such confidence—and such happiness and such a sense of having found someone who really cared whether I lived or died—that I wrote and asked her to marry me.

It was ridiculous and absurd, of course: she a famous actress, a dame, distinguished; me an under-nourished, uneducated, impecunious cockney bookseller. What impudence! Of course she wrote back to me to say she never intended to get married; but it was the sweetest, kindest letter imaginable.

Now isn't it odd that the person who has brought me most joy in my sixties is the actress who most often made me cry when I was a lad! In order to create happiness perhaps it's necessary to understand *un*happiness. And nobody who saw my beloved Flora in *For Services Rendered* thirty-seven years ago can doubt that she— above any other actress of our day—has got this wonderful understanding.

A Holiday Painter

BY J. B. PRIESTLEY

THE PIECE that follows is not addressed to professional artists, nor indeed to amateur painters who are fairly experienced. They can of course read it to amuse themselves, but they must not blame me if they are not amused. The people I have in mind as readers here are those who have wondered about starting to paint or those who have convinced themselves they could never even make a start. Over and over again, visitors to my house have said to me, 'I wish I could do that.' To which I have replied, 'Perhaps you could.' 'Oh no,' they cry, 'I know I couldn't possibly do anything like that.' 'But how do you know,' I say, 'if you've never tried?'

I must have been at least sixty when I suddenly decided to do a bit of painting. If I had been living in London I might have spent some afternoons at an art school. (I *might*, though between ourselves I doubt it.) But I was living in the Isle of Wight, miles from anywhere, and I really could not afford the time to go in search of art instruction. And I had had none since I left school, well before the First War. Moreover, at school either we drew the plaster heads of Julius Caesar and Voltaire or we designed wallpaper, under the supervision of an art master rather too fond of glaring and shouting.

Sensibly enough, I think now, I began with the usual uninspiring groups of cigar boxes, bottles, oranges and bananas. I remember once looking out of the window of my study, on a rather high first floor, and making a desperate attempt to paint what I saw out there. The result was such an appalling shambles that I felt I would never be able to tackle a landscape, which is what I wanted to do. I did not realise then that it takes time, at least a little experience, before the eye and the brush begin to sort things out together. The little still-life group *asks* to be painted; it has been created for that purpose. But a landscape exists in its own right, and you have to learn to see that it is paintable. I mention this so that fellow dabblers, also after landscapes, will not give up too easily.

A Holiday Painter

For the first few years I used both oils and watercolours, and I have a few things, just a few, in both media that I am not entirely ashamed of. But when I largely stopped painting at home, chiefly because only my afternoons were free and I had to take some exercise, and did almost all my painting when I was abroad on holiday, I discarded both oils and watercolours. I did this for two quite different sets of reasons. I felt capable of tackling landscape in oils, within my own narrow limits, but the gear was too heavy to take on long plane journeys, and apt to be too messy for hotel bedrooms. So they were out. Watercolours are of course perfect for travelling, but they are too difficult for an impatient bumbling old dauber. I have a genuine love of fine watercolours, and live with some noble specimens of the art—a Cotman, a Girtin (early-ish though), Francis Towne, Varley, De Wint, and a few good later men. But I had started laying on washes forty-five years too late; the medium was altogether too tricky; and there were enough bad watercolours about without my adding to them. So they were out too.

I settled for gouaches, have used nothing else for the last nine or ten years, and I advise any beginner, especially if he or she is a holiday painter, to follow my example. They are as light and convenient as watercolours but are not such a dangerous hit-or-miss medium. They allow you to correct your mistakes and do not condemn you to use the white of the paper as a highlight. (I use tinted paper, and after some experience you can make the colour of the paper do a lot of work for you.) They have of course their snags, and I think any brilliant performer would naturally prefer oils or watercolours. They dry very quickly and are hard to work with in a really hot country. (I have used them in Singapore, India, Peru, Morocco, Mexico, Guatemala, Trinidad, so I ought to know.) They set darker than you intended, and so are apt to be too low in tone. They are very difficult to blend and melt into each other, and you have to work fast (which suits me), so that very often, doing skies, it is better to abandon your brushes and use your fingertips, working like a maniac. This suits me too because, strictly speaking, I *am* a maniac or I would not be attempting the thing at all.

My daughters, who like to encourage the old man at Christmas or on birthdays, have presented me with various new substitutes for gouaches, paints made out of plastics, rubber, milk, God knows what. A grateful father, I have always given these substitutes a trial, but I am afraid I have soon abandoned them. I am sure they have their uses but for my kind of painting they achieve the wrong look somehow, as if you were trying to create a real shop and always ended with a super-market. So back I go, either to the French (when possible) or to Winsor & Newton.

Paper of good quality is very important for gouaches. Away from large cities it is almost impossible to find, and this has meant that on most painting holidays I have had to take an adequate supply of good paper with me, almost always in airplanes. Now the best paper, which is comparatively thick, can be a fairly heavy item in your luggage when you are taking perhaps fifty pieces of it. Now and again I have tried to save weight by taking thinner sheets, and I have always regretted it afterwards. (Why do it again, then? Because I keep thinking I have found a lighter paper that is equally good. I won't be taught by experience.) I have a good portable easel but I never take it away with me. I sit on the grass or on a rock, spread my gear round me, pin the paper to a portfolio or a very light drawing board, and then make a start.

I do no preliminary drawing in pencil but go to work at once with brushes and paint. Nine times out of ten I am compelled not only by temperament but also by circumstance to work quickly. People may have taken us out in their car, or we may have hired some sort of taxi, and with either form of transport I feel I must not be too long. If my wife has made a self-drive arrangement (excellent in Ireland, very expensive in France), then we tootle along until I spot a promising place, and she leaves the car near me while she climbs the nearest hill wherever we may be, coolly defying falls and sprained ankles, wild dogs, and attempted rape. This gives me more time but I am so accustomed now to working fast that generally I have done all I propose to do before she gets back. Occasionally of course foul weather has driven me to do my painting in the car (which I dislike because I feel so cluttered up) or staring through an hotel window. The most maddening kind of day is one that looks reasonably fine but keeps releasing a little spatter of rain, just enough to ruin your paper. A big umbrella would be useful for these days, but I always feel I have enough gear to carry without loading myself with a big umbrella.

A real artist is of course never far away from pen, pencil, brush, paper, canvas, and probably never lets a day go past without working at something. (And the great men were the hardest workers of all—think of Turner!) Therefore, you can tell how far removed I am from being a real artist when I have to confess that I may go six months without touching a brush. This was not always so; I did a fair amount of work at home during my first years; but now, confining myself to holidays, I have these long gaps when I have not even taken a look at my painting gear. (And now I realise my frequent references to 'holidays' can be misleading. I have not gone all over the world simply on holiday: I have been giving lectures or getting material for a book, and generally have been professionally employed; but as the painting belongs to the holiday part of these trips, the off-duty times, I cannot help discussing it in terms of 'holidays'. However, it is no secret that I have been, throughout these painting years, an extremely hard-working writer.) One inevitable result of these long gaps, when I am having no practice, is that I am always stiff and rusty when I start again, usually wasting several precious days on sketches not worth keeping.

If there is going to be anything worth keeping, it will come later when I am still excited by the local landscape but am not quite so stiff and rusty as I was at first. Moreover, the work, such as it is, will be better still if I suddenly find myself doing it under pressure—because I've only twenty minutes before we must go or because the weather is about to turn nasty or the light is fading fast. Naturally I am always hoping that something I can be rather proud of will suddenly arrive—and I put it like that because the things I have liked best *have* arrived: I have not consciously made them, they have made themselves. And indeed, as a rule, the greater my conscious effort the worse the result. I have said more than once that really it is no use my

Mayan temple in the jungle at Tekal, in northern Guatemala

Above: a vine-growing valley in Georgia, Soviet Union
Opposite, top: Golden Canyon in Death Valley, California
Opposite, below: Ingleborough, in the Yorkshire Dales
Below: Stormy afternoon in Breconshire

Above: the Meteora in Thessaly

Below: Road in Kerry

taking trouble because I do not know what trouble to take. So, within certain limitations, I tend to let it rip.

To understand the limitations, you have to understand that my primary object is not to create works of art—nothing so grand. Faced with an unfamiliar and interesting landscape, I get bits of it down in gouache sketches more or less in the same spirit in which my fellow tourists may be taking colour photographs. They respond their way; I respond my way. I prefer my way because more of myself goes into the response, and I feel closer to the landscape and to the spirit of the place than they do. What I do has to be clearly representational (allowing for my faulty drawing) because that is the first object of the exercise. (I did some abstracts, chiefly in oils, some years ago, and one or two of them might be worse.) I want, you may say, to remind myself where I have been, and to recapture a morning here, an afternoon there, both the time and the mood. If, by chance and luck, just a glimmer of art creeps in now and again, then so much the better, but my whole approach is on a much humbler level. And I am making these points—and indeed I am writing this whole piece—not to explain myself and my elderly antics but in the hope of encouraging other people to start from scratch and follow my example. Because—and this is the point—it does not really matter a damn what other people think about what you have done, it is not even necessary to let anybody see it (though it is pleasant if a wife or a husband can follow your progress), but if you have any feeling for landscape and want somehow to *respond* to it, this is a wonderful way to do it. And it trebles the value of any holiday. You are no longer a tourist, admiring and nodding and moving on and wondering what's for dinner. You are—not to coin a phrase—*with it*. You are, in your own modest fashion, *essential man* and not just another twentieth-century consumer.

At this point I think some notes on the sketches reproduced here might be useful. Though I do not object to the presence of any of them in these pages, I must add that they do not represent my own first choices but the editor's (and he in turn is compelled to consider various editorial needs and limitations). I am if anything a colourist, certainly no draughtsman, and I have a

A Holiday Painter

special interest in skies, an interest that cannot be given much of a chance in small reproductions of this kind. In short, I am announcing that I can do—and have done—better than this, but I cannot prove it because so far I have refused invitations to exhibit my stuff in public (exhibitions are for professional artists and not for bungling old amateurs) and indeed rarely display these things even to visiting friends for fear of boring them. True, now and again I do hang up a few, though never in prominent places of honour, so that visitors if they wish can give them a glance or two, without being compelled to say anything. But now for those notes.

On page 149 is a Mayan temple—though only the top of it, of course—in the jungle at Tekal in Guatemala. The jungle is thick and there is a lot of it, so you fly in on a DC3 from Guatemala City. There are more than one of these astounding temples, and you spend several days there, parties of not more than a dozen being boarded and lodged in a rough-and-ready fashion. Guatemala itself, a country of volcanoes and lakes, is very good value, but in winter, of course, and I recommend this trip to Tekal as its high spot. As I said earlier, I use tinted paper of various shades for gouaches, and as I happened to have a few pink sheets I used one here, as I did on several other occasions in Guatemala, for no particular reason—just for the hell of it!

The next colour reproduction, on page 152, is of a sketch of Meteora in Thessaly. This is the place where there are huge fantastic rocks, which look impossible to climb. Nevertheless, monasteries were built on top of them, and you can just see one of them in my sketch. We spent some days in this strange region, and I did several sketches, some of individual rocks, others, like the one here, of a group. This one, in fact, is not my favourite as I think some of the others are more dramatic. The other colour reproduction on page 152 takes us a long way from Greece. It is a sketch of a road in western Ireland—Kerry, in fact—and I had to do it at great speed inside the car, all cluttered up, because the rain might come down at any moment. I was not really interested in the road, rather a sentimental cliché, but in the truly magnificent sky of the lowering late afternoon. And, as the politicians say, with all due respect I do not think a small reproduction begins to do justice to what, working like a madman, I managed to get down on paper. I must add that so long as it is not raining every day, the West of Ireland seems to me unmatched for variety and a constant enchantment of colour. Hurry there, my holiday painters, before it is ruined!

The lower of the monochrome reproductions on page 150 comes from the countryside I have known and loved almost all my life, the Yorkshire Dales. Anybody who knows the Dales will, I hope, recognise that this is a sketch of Ingleborough. I have had more than one painting holiday in this glorious part of the world, and, as I write this, I have already planned another—God willing, this very June. The monochrome above takes us across the world, from the West Riding to southern California. This is a sketch of a place called Golden Canyon, running out of Death Valley, that sinister region several hundred feet below sea level and one of the hottest spots on earth. (You go there in winter, of course: summer would be murderous.) What interests me about this Golden Canyon sketch is that it was done very early, within a year or so of my starting to paint. If it comes off—and I think it does, in colour—that is because the strange Death Valley landscape excited me.

The painting on page 151, 'A Stormy Afternoon in Breconshire', I had to do very quickly because I was down in a ditch by the side of a main road, with lorries and buses passing all the time. I may have been wrong but it seemed to me the only place from which I could get the particular view I wanted, so down I went, working as fast as I could to be free of that ditch. We have to take another long jump to arrive at the other painting on page 151, from South Wales to the Caucasus. This is a rather long-range view of a famous vine-growing valley in Georgia, famous throughout the Soviet Union for its wines. Georgia might have a strong claim to be considered the most romantic-looking country in the world: most of it looks as if it were originally designed as scenery for opera. The Georgians are very hospitable and great drinkers of toasts, and the night before I painted this valley I had attended one of their dinners and had drunk far, far, far too much, with the result that I crawled down in the morning to do my painting with one of the worst hangovers I ever remember. You may feel that some of my interior darkness crept into the picture, and that is possible, but apart from a few bright accents along the valley the scene itself, with its wall of dark foothills hiding all but the peaks beyond, was rather sombre—still romantic but majestical.

I will now make a final point, as a last inducement to middle-aged and elderly people to start painting for fun. What my painting has given me, among so many other things, is *an eye*. And I do not mean now an eye for pictures, I mean an eye for the world. Since I took to painting, even with all those long intervals away from a brush, the visual world has been immensely enriched. It is as if my eye had come into a fortune. I might be said to have inherited the whole round earth. So, my friends, what more do you want? Get some gear and make a start!

A Gallery of Conductors

COMMENTARY BY CHARLES REID

PHOTOGRAPHS BY ERICH AUERBACH

HISTORICALLY CONSIDERED, virtuoso conducting is an art of recent growth, little more than a century old. We are still sorting out its principles and ethics. How much showmanship may we welcome? How much 'personality cult' encourage—if any at all?

Things have changed out of knowledge in the concert hall. When Victoria was a young Queen orchestras—commonly known as 'bands', a name they shared with Christmas waits—were still conducted either by the first fiddle, who broke off playing to beat time whenever he could spare a moment, or by 'continuo', the man at the piano or harpsichord, whose job was to fill in the harmonies and extemporise twiddly bits ('cadences', 'ornaments') with his right hand. These functionaries enjoyed little social consideration; even the more cultivated and prosperous among them were expected to ring at the servants' entrance. They were superseded because of two main factors. One factor involved Beethoven.

Musicians had come to realise that the emotional depths and conundrums of the Beethoven symphonies in particular (though not Beethoven's music alone) called for more efficient co-ordination than the old routine afforded. More importantly, they called for what came to be known as 'interpretation'. It was seen there must somebody untrammelled at the top, not only to keep everybody else on the beat but also to make a Beethoven symphony hang together in performance as logically and artistically as a Beethoven piano sonata under one mind and one pair of hands.

From about the middle of the nineteenth century Beethoven's

A Gallery of Conductors

requirements were supplemented by two composers of commanding genius: Hector Berlioz and Richard Wagner. They were the second evolutionary factor. To the new-born symphony orchestra these two added a thousand undreamt-of voices, a thousand coral caves and snow peaks, a thousand enchantments that will last for as long as humans have ears to hear.

Thus was the virtuoso conductor born. He couldn't help being. He was as inevitable a product of musical expansion as the master-architect is of the progress (if it *is* that) from mud-and-wattle to tower blocks. Fittingly enough, Berlioz and Wagner were the first virtuoso conductors in history, Berlioz being the more conspicuous of the two; outside his own country, France (which was scandalously tone deaf in his regard), he won massive 'quality' ovations in which we may detect precursor symptoms of present-day conductor worship.

Most of the music Berlioz got ovations for conducting was music he had composed himself. Those who immediately followed him as rostrum virtuosos down the decades—the von Bülows, Richters, Weingartners, Nikisches, Toscaninis, Kussevitskys and such—were either 'career conductors' who didn't compose a note or composers who, having failed to be loved for their own music, raised the roof and won reverence by conducting that of their betters. Under the pressure of their virtuosity and attendant brouhaha, the orchestras who served them were sedulously trained and had more money spent on them. Every great or middling city ran up a concert hall with orchestral and choral concerts in mind. There was a great expenditure of marble. During the first phase of the conductor cult faithful audiences began to line up at box-offices, without any spur from either the gramophone (an infant still) or radio, (a) to hear the composer, (b) to see the conductor—or the other way about, according to who the conductor was and what his Glam Rating.

This last is, I know, a banal phrase. No other phrase really fits. What we must accept, whether the purists wring their hands or not, is that the conductor's psyche, to use an old-fashioned word, has been getting increasingly into the act ever since Toscanini's and Beecham's day. It wasn't merely that these two and many confrères, especially Furtwängler, took or tended to take the symphonic classics at different speeds and with different emphases. The new and imponderable factor in the race of rostrum stars was that the public delighted in their idiosyncracies: their eyes, smile, gait, gestures, hair, waggishness or profundity, cut of clothes, cut of beard (if any) and what not.

Delighting in such matters is not in the least wrong. The human mind is capable of relishing such things and, at the same time, taking in a fine performance of 'The Twilight of the Gods' or Mozart's 'Jupiter' Symphony or Beethoven's Ninth. If there are people who go to concerts solely to stare, not to listen, why make moan? They are doing no harm to anybody or anything, except perhaps their pockets.

Conductor-as-spectacle is a matter on which conductors themselves differ sharply. One school, typified by Sir Adrian Boult, believes in minimal gestures. Sir Adrian is given to expounding how well a choral-orchestral ensemble can be directed in some contexts with the right arm held practically still and the wrist held five inches from the chest, the baton being manipulated solely by the fingers. His older contemporary, the late Sir Henry Wood, the venerated founder of the London Promenade Concerts, took a different line. Wood was given to extolling 'the *art* [my italics] of gesture'. 'Don't be scared of exhibiting your temperaments', he counselled his conducting pupils in effect. He made no bones about sending them to the ballet for tips on how to use their hands and arms to the most eloquent effect.

Wood's idea was that an intelligent conductor's uninhibited movements, while lucidly directing the performers in front of him, could, up to a point, 'portray' the music's moods and fundamental purport to those behind his back who had paid at the doors. He, for one, was not afraid of letting himself go. 'I always say I *paint the picture* with my baton', he used to boast—not without reason. He never outflung an arm or led a *fortissimo* charge, baton upraised, without a commensurate technical point in view. His exuberance was splendid for its own sake, however. After all, music is something to exuberate about. 'Timber' lashing about in the opening movement of Tchaikovsky's Symphony No. 4 at the point where the masonry of cities topples to chaos was a musico-visual one treasures. Beecham did the same kind of thing a bit more theatrically. At the height of some brassy tumult in Strauss's *Ein Heldenleben* he appeared to fire a furious Colt .45 at the trombones. He frowned. He glowed anger. Through the thick of Straussian *tutti* he bawled his troops on to victory. It was appalling form. It didn't always conduce to a good performance. We wouldn't readily have gone without it, though.

The two schools of virtuoso conductors are still with us—still in conflict. We will call them the Reticents and the Florids. There can be no doubt which is the better box-office.

WITHOUT academic pass-outs of any kind, Sir Thomas Beecham gave British music the most salutary shake-up in its history. There were early piano lessons at home. While writing dud operas and conducting scratch outfits he had composition lessons from the odd pundit. These didn't count. What counted were three things. First: a musical memory which, at the start, was like electronic tape. Second: his father's money, the 'Beecham Pill' fortune. On the first (1909) of his three symphony orchestras and his early theatre seasons he spent the equivalent of £1,500,000 in today's money. Third: a barbed, uproarious tongue. He told his audiences they were ninnies. They loved him for it. At Covent Garden he had them cheering Strauss's *Elektra* and *Salome*, pieces they couldn't make head nor tail of. Really the cheers were for 'Tommy' himself. The gallery was calling him that before the Kaiser's War. When he died fifty years later he was 'Tommy' to the nation at large. Connoisseurs will never forget the sunlit suavity of his Mozart, the iridescence of his Delius, the weight and verve of his Berlioz.

ONE VIRTUOSO in our gallery breaks all virtuoso rules—
except the musical ones. Sir Adrian Boult's psyche is of
no consequence to Sir Adrian. He is one of the Rostrum
Reticents. He has done great things. At forty he built the BBC
Symphony Orchestra, picking the players, training them, conducting them in-chief for twenty years. Who will forget his 1936
concert version of Alban Berg's formidable *Wozzeck*? At that time
Wozzeck scared the daylights out of every other eminent conductor
in the land. Berg listened in—and sent Boult a letter of lyrical
praise, pages long.

No virtuoso has earned more thunderous applause. It does not
interest him. He has often stepped down and walked away from it.
Basking in applause is 'the sort of thing one doesn't do. That is why',
he has said, 'I prefer to conduct in cathedrals. They can't applaud
there.' Or couldn't. They do nowadays in St Paul's. Is no place safe?

WHEN SIR MALCOLM SARGENT took calls at the end of a concert there were stars of adoration in women's eyes. It would be going far to say no other conductor was so greatly loved. What may be said is that no other conductor was loved with the same *élan* or touch of surrender. The other conductors bristled or scoffed. Beecham called him 'the idol of the bus conductresses'. His psyche was of the irresistible sort. It brought thousands to music, or made them feel it more deeply. Ovations he prized, partly because he was in essence a lonely man and needed heart-warming, partly because they enhanced the prestige of choirs and orchestras. Orchestral players who, in general, knocked his musicianship ('too fussy', 'over-rigid') liked him for this. His *Messiah* and B minor Mass differed from most others because he believed in what the words said. This set a special seal upon his performances which many miss.

H<small>E WAS BAPTISED</small> Giovanni Batista Barbirolli, son and grandson of immigrant violinists who once shared first desk in the opera pit at Rovigo, Italy. His mother was French. He has no drop of English blood; inherited a dislike of strong sunlight; has been known to shutter himself against it even in the North; conducts Elgar, whose music is as English as the Union flag, with the loyalty, insight and fervour proper to an 'adoptee'. Once he played 'cello in silent cinema, opera and even pantomime pits, as well as in chamber music and (brilliantly) on recital platforms. After conducting Toscanini's old orchestra, the New York Philharmonic (1936–43), Sir John opted for Manchester, most English of cities; and he remained true to its Hallé Orchestra (he is now its Conductor Laureate) against proffered plum appointments from orchestral managements in two continents.

164

Pierre Monteux was born in a Paris still scarred from the street fighting of 1871; lived into the age of cooked-up electronic music; was told two years before his death (1964) that he had the blood pressure of a young man; at that time still conducted on his feet even in recording studios where he could have sat. 'How', he asked, 'can the boys be expected to concentrate if I loll back?' When seventy-six he was given a banquet in the U.S. After set speeches he rose to make 'a solemn declaration: my hair is not dyed'. His name belongs to history for conducting the first night of Stravinsky's *Rite of Spring* through hullabaloo and near-riot (Paris 1913). He stayed loyal to *The Rite*, doing over fifty performances of it, against personal dislike— '*Je suis tué par ce rhythme là.*' He talked jocosely of doing it on his hundredth birthday. He died with eleven years to go. Even the Monteux of this world come to an end.

AT EIGHTEEN Bruno Walter conducted *Pagliacci* in a gaslit theatre, Altona, Germany. Wide, vigorous beat. Banged his hands often and blisteringly on lamp cowls flanking his desk. In mid-career, as Bavarian Court conductor, wore knee breeches, sword, cocked hat to regal ceremonies. Suffered racial persecution by Nazis. Fled to the U.S. At seventy returned to Europe for the Indian Summer of a crammed, noble career. Its noblest aspect: fervent and lifelong championship of Mahler's music.

L EOPOLD STOKOWSKI, son of a Polish immigrant, won spurs as a young church organist in London. At twenty-two he was conducting the Cincinnati orchestra; at twenty-five the Philadelphia. After that the world was his parish. In his eighth decade he was still conducting. He spurns the baton. Instead he uses his hands—with signal elegance and precision. His silver mane and a profile of the sort engraved on antique coins are in themselves enough to ensure a sell-out wherever he goes.

IN TWENTY YEARS Ernest Ansermet made some two hundred 'long play' records for one label, the last when he was eighty-five. An exceptional score argues an exceptional following. Yet, conducting in many lands, he never obsessed the public eye. As a young man he had taught mathematics in his native Switzerland. But music was an encroaching hobby. During the Kaiser's War he became a conductor and was taken up by Stravinsky, who, between 1918 and 1930, gave him the premières of two theatre pieces (*The Soldier's Tale* and *Reynard*), the *Capriccio* for piano and orchestra and the *Symphony of Psalms*. At thirty-five he founded l'Orchestre de la Suisse romande. With it he recorded himself to fame.

SIXTY YEARS AGO in Germany a young coach prepared the finale-chorus of Mahler's 'Resurrection' Symphony for performance, then transcribed the whole work for piano *con amore*. Touched and impressed, Mahler wrote a line or two on a card recommending Otto Klemperer (opposite), to whomsoever might be interested, as 'a predestined conductor'. The decades that followed were arduous and stormy. He compiled a massive repertory of operas and symphonies; brought a lawsuit against politicos of the Weimar Republic on musical subsidy issues; and, being a Jew, was hounded into exile by the Nazis. Then a sequence of physical blows. A brain-tumour operation left him paralysed down one side; a fall broke his leg on the other side; at seventy-three he suffered severe burns accidentally. Thrice his career seemed at full close. Thrice he renewed it. At eighty-three Klemperer is still unconquered.

During his first thirty professional years, i.e. up to the mid-1960s, Rudolf Kempe mastered a hundred operas and gave 1,870 performances of them, mainly in his native Germany. He has a platform repertory of five hundred pieces; and conducts a quarter of them from memory. Covent Garden connoisseurs were head over heels about his *Ring* (Wagner) cycles, 1954–8. He has conducted eighty crack orchestras; like Barbirolli, he knows them from inside. For eight years he was an oboist.

TAKING his first rehearsal with a leading London orchestra when twenty-two, Benjamin Britten was openly derided by the players because they didn't think much of the piece he was putting them through, his symphonic cycle, *Our Hunting Fathers*. On the night, however, they gave him a first-class performance. This for a simple reason. As has been shown since on many platforms and recording floors, he is a first-class baton. Characteristically he thinks his conducting not up to much.

THE POST-WAR DECADES threw up two conductors of a type without precedent or parallel except, perhaps, in that sector of industry or commerce where a single enterprise breeds swarming subsidiaries and there is no stop on the number of directorships that may be hidden under one hat. At this writing Leonard Bernstein (above), b. Lawrence, Mass., is fifty years old. Herbert von Karajan (opposite), b. Salzburg, Austria, is sixty. Between them they have conducted more orchestras, directed more musical institutions and kept more artistic irons in the fire than six ordinary citizens could cope with in a lifetime.

Bernstein's is the more faceted talent. He guested with the New York Philharmonic Orchestra first at the age of twenty-five, as stand-in for the indisposed Bruno Walter. During ten years and a bit (1958–69), as the N.Y.P.'s musical director, he toured them tirelessly: Jerusalem to Tokyo, West Berlin to Moscow. In and among he guested with sixteen other crack orchestras in seven countries. At the Scala, Milan, he conducted Maria Callas in Cherubini's *Medea*, at the Vienna State Opera Fischer-Dieskau in *Falstaff* (Verdi); 'professed' music for five years at an American university; and sold a hundred thousand copies of his book *The Joy of Music* in next to no time. It was this same Bernstein who composed *West Side Story*, *On the Town*, *Wonderful Town* and *Candide*, hits one and all. *And* a mass of serious music. He has three symphonies to his name. . . . One could go on.

Von Karajan's special gift is for being the lord of several manors at once. Serving his apprenticeship in minor German opera houses in the late 1920s and under the Nazis, he was ensconced at the Berlin State Opera during Hitler's war. It was in the late 1940s and mid–1950s that manors fell into his lap. The Vienna Philharmonic and Berlin Philharmonic orchestras became his. So did Salzburg Festival and the Vienna State Opera. At Bayreuth he conducted *Tristan* and *Der Ring*. The Philharmonia of London is among foreign orchestras for whom he was breath-of-nostrils. Somebody dubbed him King Emperor of European Music. A tiring office. Latterly he has cut down on his sway a little, for health reasons. But the biggest manor of all is opening up. In Japan he and his Berlin orchestra had a television audience (so it was claimed) of thirty-two million. He scoffs at traditional 2,000-capacity auditoriums. It seems that colour film, endless miles of it, is the way to the musical enrichment of the masses. If things work out as von Karajan envisages, King Emperor will be more imperial than ever.

AT TWENTY-SIX George Solti, a Karlsruhe Opera coach, was sacked because he was a Jew (Hungarian) and went back to Budapest. Having conducted one *Figaro* there, he was shooed away by Nazi-slanted edicts and spent the war in Switzerland. He had to bottle up his musical energies for fourteen years. His musical directorships of the Bavarian State, Frankfurt and Covent Garden operas from 1946 on, plus his guesting with leading European orchestras, gave him tempestuous release. It does not do to call him a dynamo. He is a power station. Whether a power station ought really to conduct Mozart is questionable. *Der Ring* is another matter. In this, as Solti took it, many of us revelled. Not that it was better than Kempe's. It was merely that the time had come for a dynamic change. And his Covent Garden *Moses and Aaron* (Schoenberg) shook the opera-going world.

COLIN DAVIS began as a freelance clarinet player; had a spell in the Glyndebourne Opera pit; played an excruciating wrong note at a *Così fan tutte* dress rehearsal. He graduated to top-baton at Sadler's Wells Opera; is now chief of the BBC Symphony Orchestra and musical-director-elect of the Royal Opera House (Covent Garden). These appointments all happened in just over eight years. His three great musical passions are Mozart, Berlioz, Stravinsky, for the second and third of whom he has done much. Like Henry Wood, he believes in showing his musical feelings. When he wants a *pianissimo* he gives at the knees and screws up his face small. At rehearsal he says picturesque things. Thus, of a bassoon entry in a Mozart slow movement: 'Here comes the *poison note*. Always in Mozart you get the touch of poison, the shadow on felicity.' He's a James Joyce reader, and sounds like it.

A book of Erich Auerbach's photographs of musicians, AN EYE FOR MUSIC, *will be published next year.*

JAMES BLADES, from the film *We Make Music* (World Mirror Productions)

The Man behind the Drums BY JAMES BLADES

A MUSIC CRITIC once said that I lived by calculated violence done to a variety of instruments. To this intriguing description by John Amis of the professional side of an orchestral percussionist's vocation could be added the task of calculating periods of silence to a split second, for it is at times far more difficult to do nothing than to do something. A count of 209 bars' rest instead of Wagner's prescribed 210 preceding the entry of the first mighty clash of cymbals in the Mastersingers Overture—and you're for it!

A life behind the drums may seem to some a strange occupation, and possibly precarious. It could be both, but on the other hand it can be full of excitement and very rewarding. Like most professional players I've often been asked what prompted me to become 'pro' and why I chose percussion. Well, I just wanted to play the drum, and I must confess that it was no classical masterpiece that inspired me to make music. No, it was the sound of a bass drum—the big drum in a Salvation Army Band.

At the age of seven or so, Sunday evening usually found me on Peterborough Market Place as near as possible to the man who played the big drum. To me he was the star performer in the band. He was an ex-Guards drummer named Jim Pack—a fine big man and a tremendous showman on the march, with his stick-twirling, etc. Exciting as was his pyrotechnic display, it was the soft sounds he made in the hymns that thrilled me most. Gentle rumbling like distant thunder, with sometimes a crescendo into the last verse which would nearly lift me off my feet. Many a time I was brought back to earth by the sound of the five-minute bell sounding from the church nearby where I was a probationer chorister. What a scutter it was for me to get into the vestry in time for the processional!

In addition to the Salvation Army bass drum there was the lure of Uncle George's drumsticks. Uncle George did a bit of drumming in the Volunteers Band, and on Sunday mornings

The Man behind the Drums

after service I called on Uncle George and Auntie Lydia hoping for one thing to be asked to stay to dinner. Auntie 'Liddy' made marvellous Yorkshire puddings—and big helpings too. Whilst Auntie was busy in the kitchen, Uncle and I would get down to business in the front room: he tapping on a leather chair in time with his gramophone, and I trying to imitate Mr Pack's bass drum by thumping on a cushion. What a time we had! But invariably Auntie put an end to our performance by boxing our ears and saying it was a Sunday, and come in and get your dinner.

Uncle George was determined that I should really play the drums. When he returned from France in 1918 he began to teach me the necessary rudiments for the side drum: paradiddles, stroke rolls, etc., ensuring that I did plenty of Mam-my—Dad-dy practice—the accelerating two beats on each hand to produce the long roll.

The hallmark of an orchestral side drummer is a smooth well-controlled roll: the technical term for a sustained note or tremolo on all percussion instruments. To cultivate and maintain a smooth roll entirely free of rhythmical stresses requires assiduous practice. The same applies to the numerous rudiments which include grace notes, such as flams and drags. Some of the solos given to the side drum in the orchestral repertoire are particularly taxing. A touch of the 'pearlies' (a nervous tremble), and the solo to open Ravel's *Bolero* 'goes for a Burton'! Similarly the solo side-drum rolls which open the overture to Rossini's *La Gazza Ladra*—the first *forte* and the second usually played *pp* as an echo. No one was more aware of the concern of the side drummer at this point than Sir Thomas Beecham. If he was in a particularly whimsical mood he would start the player on the *pp* roll, and then turn to his leader or another acquaintance and chat for what seemed to the side drummer the length of the overture! One of *my* most trying experiences was sustaining a roll for three minutes to cover a situation in a horror film. Here my early practice stood me in good stead.

I became something of a nuisance at home with my constant 'tip-tap', and I was given the pigsty as my practice den. Our pig was spared the infliction, having been eaten the previous winter.

Uncle George eventually arranged for two local players to take me in hand, and I soon qualified sufficiently to do an odd job in small dance bands, augmenting slightly my meagre wage as an apprentice engineer.

My musical chum at this time was a youth named Frank Hitchborn, a pianist. As we were not overwhelmed with paid engagements we decided to form an orchestra. For some reason or other no one seemed anxious to team up with us, so we formed a duo—piano and drums. The magnificence of this combination, and the fact that we were at liberty for weddings, dances, and suchlike occasions, we made known to all and sundry; but we remained unaccountably 'vacant'. Then something happened. Our town was to have a visit from Royalty: the Prince of Wales was to open the Agricultural Show. The great day arrived, and Frank and I obtained a good position near the show ground—just as we had planned—he with a melodium borrowed from his grandfather, and I with a small drum. As the procession, headed by the Prince and City Officials, passed us we struck up 'God Bless the Prince of Wales', or something resembling it. We were immediately grabbed by a policeman who jerked us to the back of the crowd and rebuked us in no uncertain terms. A night in jail would not have worried us; our object had been achieved. We made our way quickly to a stationer's shop and ordered cards to be printed—'Played before Royalty'!

Frank and I did a little better after this, but it was still a difficult business getting known, and my aim was to become a professional. To become a 'pro' when I was a young man was a tough proposition, and in the majority of cases a start was made in a small and often insecure way. Things are different today: young people are given every opportunity at school to study musical instruments, and there is the school or youth orchestra, followed by a year or two at one of the colleges or academies. After that—if they prove worthy—there is every chance of a place in a professional orchestra.

My first job was in a circus band. I replied to an advertisement in *The Era*, and received an offer written on a piece of fish-and-chip paper which read: 'Start Monday, Ginnetts Circus, Henley-on-Thames, £3 a week and tent—Sam'. I got the tent, but never the

The Man behind the Drums

three pounds! As things were now mighty slack in the engineering industry I had little difficulty in getting released from my indentures. With the blessing of my family and Frank, and a sigh of relief from the neighbours, I made my way to Henley-on-Thames and found the band tent that was to be my home for the next three months. Sam—of the fish-and-chip paper—turned out to be the bandmaster. He eyed me up and down, and so did a lion in a nearby cage, but both turned out to be quite friendly chaps. Sam told me we started at three o'clock and gave me some bits of music, which I must confess looked like Greek to me, particularly the opening march. But I was certain of one thing: at the start I was to play for two bars, then count two bars rest, and then start the drumming again.

At three o'clock Sam started us off by nodding his elbow (he played a cornet as well as conducted). I went: 'Pom-tiddy-pom-tiddy-pom-pom-pom' and counted softly 'one-two-two-two'. 'Stop,' yelled Sam to the other men—all three of them (second cornet, trombone and euphonium). Sam turned to me and shouted: 'What the so-and-so do you think you're doing?' I replied in a quaking voice: 'Two bars rest, sir.' He said: 'Now look here, my boy, circus drummers never ruddy well rest; from the time we start to the time we finish you flog them drums as hard as you can go.' That single experience was worth a fortune; it taught me that the conductor is always right!

I survived my next engagement by sheer diplomacy. It was in a small silent cinema. The manager told me not to bother about the music but to watch the screen, and the conductor told me to watch the music and not to bother about the screen! For some time I found it easier to heed the manager. The conductor would angrily point at the music, to which I replied by pointing to the screen and the manager's office. In due course the drum music became less puzzling, and I neglected the screen occasionally and thereby pleased the conductor. Down would come the manager and point to the screen, and I would then point to the conductor. I kept the two of them at bay, practised hard, and saved enough money to buy my first pair of timpani.

The men in the orchestra impressed on me the value of getting experience by moving around. I got work in various parts of the country: Jarrow, Workington and Dundee. It was in Dundee that I did my first broadcast—a few simple tunes on the xylophone in a tea-time programme. I also had the interesting experience of officiating as an organ-stop. A rival cinema installed a massive Wurlitzer complete with all the gadgets. Our organ had no such accoutrements, so the manager (a resourceful man) decided that I should be installed in the bowels of the organ complete with glockenspiel, xylophone and tubular bells. Working from a red light which flashed when the organist pulled out a dummy stop, we kept the opposition in hand until we beat them with a larger Wurlitzer.

My experience as an organ-stop did me no end of good. The snippets I played on the glockenspiel, xylophone, etc., needed a good deal of practice, inasmuch as the majority of them had to be memorised. Until such composers as Bartók, much of the writing for the xylophone and similar instruments was repetitive and imitative, and consisted of short passages often memorised. In recent years there has been a marked change in the style of writing for the tuned percussion (glockenspiel, xylophone, marimba, vibraphone and tubular bells or chimes). The complex and often lengthy passages can be difficult to memorise. Today it is essential that the tuned percussion player is an able sight-reader. In most cases he is a specialist and is responsible for the more important of the parts given to the xylophone, etc. To watch the music, the instrument, and the conductor is no mean feat. An expert player is in great demand and is much appreciated by the powers that be. On one occasion when conducting the BBC Symphony Orchestra Toscanini halted proceedings to congratulate Stephen Whittaker (a lifelong colleague of mine) on his expertise on the glockenspiel.

In comparison with Steve's prowess my efforts in the organ loft must have been pretty mediocre; but it was good groundwork for what was to follow. My chief concern was to get to London. Through the good services of the late George Black (of the London Palladium), for whom I had worked in the Newcastle area, I eventually got to London, the Crouch End Empire, then a silent cinema. During the first afternoon matinée nineteen pianists gave auditions, leaving the conductor little time to notice what I was doing. Possibly not a bad effort, for as I left the cinema after the evening performance a fellow tapped me on the shoulder and said *sotto voce*: 'Are you the drummer?' I replied, 'Yes'. He said: 'How much are they paying you?' 'Five pounds eight a week,' I replied. 'I'll give you six quid at Clapton Rink,' he said.

Having got to London, my aim was to get into the West End. Again George Black was helpful, fixing me at the Holborn Empire. Here I played under a typical variety hall conductor, Sam Richardson—a mixture of brutality and kindliness. He frightened the life out of me with his big cigar and white gloves; but, as others had done, I soon grew to love and admire him. Six months of twice-nightly programmes (fourteen acts, most of them with an effects cue sheet as long as your arm:—'Catch me as I fall', 'Motor horn when he taps me on the bottom', etc., etc.) convinced me that this was not altogether my sort of music.

Dance bands still fascinated me, and they were considered good jobs too. An engagement of this nature came my way, admittedly out of London, but at quite a swell hotel: The Majestic, St. Annes-on-Sea, with Gerald Bright (later the famous Geraldo). Gerald Bright was a model of sartorial elegance, quite the most handsome leader I have met, and (omitting his sarcasm) one of the nicest. He took a ghoulish delight, however, in pouncing on me to play the opening of *Tales from the Vienna Woods* on my newly acquired vibraphone, knowing that the 'double-stopping' (chords), combined with the pedalling system —similar to the sustaining pedal on the piano—gave me a good deal of trouble. The vibraphone—an American invention—was at that time (1929) a recent arrival in England, functioning primarily in light music. It was not until 1934 that this instrument attracted serious composers. Berg is generally given as having first scored for it (*Lulu*, 1934). The bars of the vibraphone are made from a metal alloy. Unlike the xylophone and the marimba, where the tube resonators below each wooden bar merely strengthen the note, the resonating tubes on the vibraphone act as pulsators. The tube is opened and closed at the top by means of small fans or shutters which are revolved by motor mechanism. The breaking up of the air column alternately strengthens and weakens the sound of each bar; hence the vibrato.

The present world of swing can boast of some phenomenal vibraphonists, e.g. Milt Jackson and Gary Burton. Such experts may have been inspired by the performances of such great players as Red Norvo and Lionel Hampton.

Following my stay at the Hotel Majestic came two delightful years with Al Davison and his Claribel Band: the summers at the Villa Marina, Douglas, I.O.M., and the winters trotting round London providing musical interludes six times daily between the recently introduced 'talkies'. Al Davison was a superb musician and scholar, and possessed the most placid temperament. On the one occasion when he tried to lose his temper—during a rehearsal of Gershwin's *Rhapsody in Blue* with Al as the soloist—the attempt proved such a miserable failure that he halted the rehearsal and took us all out for a drink! I know of no musician who did not profit stylistically and otherwise from contact with Al Davison.

Al did more for me than improve my knowledge of the progressions so necessary in the current style of improvising on the vibraphone and xylophone. He released me—with his blessing—from a contract at the Dominion Theatre, Tottenham Court Road, where the Claribel Band was accompanying Jeannette Macdonald in a spectacular stage presentation, to enable me to accept the offer of a West End 'plum'—behind the drums at the Piccadilly Hotel. Here, with Gerry Hoey and his six-piece dance band, I remained for ten years, every one of them full of excitement and hard work. Soon after settling down at the Piccadilly I became house-drummer at the Gaumont British Film Studios with Louis Levy. This led to similar positions at Denham (London Films with Muir Mathieson), Elstree Studios with Idris Lewis, and Ealing Studios with the redoubtable Ernest Irving. Added to this was a fair number of gramophone sessions with such personalities as Tauber, John McCormack, Gracie Fields and Peter Dawson, and such unusual experiences as deputising for a famous cimbalom player on the roof garden of a house in Mayfair on the occasion of an élite luncheon party, when, dressed

The Man behind the Drums

as a Magyar, I performed elaborate variations—based largely on Al Davison's famous 'busking formulas'—on a vibraphone discreetly veiled in blue velvet. My expertise was highly applauded by the assembled guests, few of whom were sober, though the members of the orchestra (none of whom spoke English) were by no means so enthusiastic, and viewed me with grave suspicion.

Most days started at or before 10 a.m. and finished in the small hours, an average week being sixty-five hours wielding the drumsticks or keeping alert to do so at any prescribed moment. (During '39–'45 eighty working hours was not unusual.)

Long as the hours were, there was no hint of boredom—one never knew what to expect next. On one occasion I returned home at about my usual time (3 a.m.) to learn that Louis Levy had phoned at midnight to say that the effect of a horse with a loose shoe was required for the morrow's film. That meant an hour or so in my workshop experimenting with coconut shells and so forth. The 'cloppidy-clink' worked wonderfully well on the recording, compensating for the reduction in my usual glorious four and a half hours' sleep.

Life at the Piccadilly Hotel was equally exciting and surprisingly relaxing. What was required here was quiet 'mushy' dance music, known to the 'pro' as the 'West End drone'. Diversion came by way of two short cabarets and an occasional stunt to amuse the customers. The majority of these jokes were impromptu, but our New Year's Eve presentation was a carefully planned affair. On one occasion Gerry (the leader) suggested that we rig up our double-bass player as Father Time. Here was an excellent idea, and after a good deal of consideration it was agreed that Bill—complete with beard, wig and scythe—should be secreted inside a huge grandfather clock case that I managed to pick up in Shepherd's Bush market. It was arranged that the clock, complete with Bill, be shuffled to the front of the band rostrum at a little before midnight, and Bill would work the hours of the clock face from the inside. Midnight on the clock face was to be my cue to play the chimes of Big Ben, and on the twelfth stroke Bill was to emerge through the front door of the clock and announce the New Year. At rehearsal the whole thing went like a bomb, and we were all certain that we were on a winner.

At a few minutes to midnight the lights were lowered and the clock was duly placed in position. 'Zepp', the head waiter, gave me the tip as the hour reached midnight. I chimed the four quarters and started to strike twelve; but then the trouble started. Instead of the door opening slowly as we had arranged I heard Bill scratching about inside the clock, and it was soon obvious that he had got hooked up somehow or could not find the catch in the dark. I slowed the strokes on the bells and hoped for the best. As I struck twelve, the door of the clock burst open with a terrific crash, and Bill shot out halfway across the ballroom floor, falling on his scythe and breaking it in half. Disaster! —or so it seemed. Bill, however, was a resourceful chap. Up he jumped, shouted: 'Out with the old,' and dashed the remainder of his scythe on the floor. 'In with the new,' he yelled, as he threw his beard and wig to the 'customers'. It was a riot. Bill took umpteen calls, I nipped in with a drum roll, and off we went into *Auld Lang Syne*, during which Mr Jacoby, the manager, grabbed Gerry's hand and said: 'Gerry my boy, this was the best ever—how did you think it all out!'

That episode heralded 1939, and by the following New Year's Eve I was engaged with material of a sterner nature. I made two trips to France in October 1939 with the first Ensa troop of the war. The party was headed by Sir Seymour Hicks and included Gracie Fields and Tom Webster (of 'Tishy' fame). I left the Piccadilly Hotel to become a member of the London Symphony Orchestra. Ensa concerts with this famous orchestra, work in the film studios, and a tremendous amount of broadcasting more than filled each day. It fell to my lot to record the 'V' signal drum beats for the BBC. My association with this signal (possibly one of the most widely heard sounds in the history of radio), and the fact that I recorded the sound of the gong which is the audible signal of the Rank Organisation, have made me (somewhat against my will) something of a legend in certain circles.

On many occasions during the war I had sudden calls to fill a gap in many of our leading orchestras, conducted at that time by such notabilities as Sir Henry Wood, Sir Adrian Boult, the then Dr Malcolm Sargent, Albert Coates, George Weldon, Basil Cameron, and of course 'Sir Thomas'. On one occasion I

The Man behind the Drums

had an urgent call to join the London Philharmonic Orchestra at Oxford. I arrived at the Sheldonian almost on the 'downbeat'! The principal percussionist, Freddie (Bonzo) Bradshaw, greeted me and said: 'We covered everything as well as we could at rehearsal. Take the triangle, tambourine and bass drum, and nip in on anything else you can as we are a man short.' He added: 'Not too close a roll on the tambourine in the 'Tame Bear' (*Wand of Youth Suite*) as it's supposed to sound like a chain.' 'Keep the triangle down in the *Enigma*, Variation II—it's the tinkle of the medal on Dan the dog's collar—and plenty of bass drum in the finale. Keep an eye on Sir Adrian, he won't let you down.' I kept an eye on Sir Adrian, and he kept one on me too—as he has done a few times since!

The playing of such instruments as the triangle and tambourine may appear to be a simple undertaking. Not in a symphony orchestra, by any means. Such instruments, and indeed every percussion instrument, is a solo voice, and nerves of steel are required at every entry, be it *ppp* or *fff*. Even more so with the timpanist—the maestro of the orchestral percussion section who, in addition to the demarcation of rhythm, joins the harmony of the orchestra. The orchestral timpanist is judged by his tone, intonation and technical command. The apparently simple parts given to the timpani in the works of such early composers as Bach, Haydn and Mozart are no less exacting than the intricacies in many *avant-garde* compositions, as pitch, tone and precision are vital in every instance. The timpanist's task is aptly described by Dr Gordon Jacob who says: 'A conductor is always thankful for the presence of a really reliable timpanist. His part in the orchestra is so telling and individual, especially in modern works, that he is looked upon as an important soloist in the orchestra and one who can contribute both rhythmical firmness and dramatic excitement to an interpretation.' These aspects are similarly necessary in the works of Beethoven, as for example the four gentle strokes to open the Violin Concerto, or the tremendous energy required throughout the Ninth Symphony. The works of Mahler are equally demanding, and this could be said of many of the works of such composers as Berlioz, Bartók, Stravinsky, Bliss, Walton and Britten.

Of all the instruments of percussion, none are more satisfying to play than the kettledrums, though all members of the orchestral 'kitchen' are involved in moments of excitement, and at times danger. I recall an occasion at the Royal Albert Hall, during the first of the Christmas series of carol concerts given by the Royal Choral Society. The massive choir was accompanied by the late Arnold Greir (organ), William Bradshaw (timpani and chimes) and myself (cymbals and other percussion), with Sir Malcolm Sargent at the helm. My great moment was a mighty clash on the cymbals at the beginning of 'The First Nowell'. It was a beauty, but, to my horror, what I thought was 'Nowell' proved to be an encore of 'Silent Night'! I was duly sent for and admonished. In apologising I pleaded the fact of having been overwhelmed by the occasion, to which Sir Malcolm replied, somewhat icily, that it had indeed been a great occasion.

Repartee with Sir Malcolm and such notabilities could be suicidal, though the 'baton' was not always the victor, as for example when a well-known oboist placed Sir Thomas at a disadvantage. The oboist (James McDonagh, father of the eminent Terence) had replied with his customary Irish wit to a thrust from Sir Thomas. 'Ah,' said Sir Thomas, 'we have a fool at the end of the oboe.' 'Which end, Sir Thomas?' replied 'Mac', pointing the bell of his instrument at Sir Thomas.

Moments such as this break the tension of exhaustive rehearsals in the symphony world. The pressure in the recording and film studio is often relieved by an outburst, or a spot of practical fun. The film studio in particular has produced many colourful characters. The genial Muir Mathieson, Louis Levy—a martinet with his 'settle down' and 'more morendo', and the redoubtable Ernest Irving. Louis Levy was considered to be something of a tyrant; in comparison with Ernest Irving he was a turtle dove. Irving had the reputation of being able to play two games of chess and win them both, and conduct (or misconduct) a musical performance at the same time. Like that grand musician Walter Goehr, who had the habit of addressing you as 'Dr' if he knew you were in difficulty, Ernest Irving was invincible, or nearly so.

I may have broken even with Ernest Irving over a bell stroke

The Man behind the Drums

in the title music of a film dealing with the life of Handel. For reason of acoustics I was placed with the choir—away from the orchestra. After considerable rehearsal we got down to the business of 'taking'. My first bell stroke occurred on the 25th bar of the piece. I had no sooner struck the bell than Ernest stopped the orchestra with a shout that nearly shook the sopranos off the platform. He turned to me and said: 'You came in a bar too early with the bell.' I apologised, but Ernest was in one of his moods. 'You're not convinced,' he said. I made a non-committal reply. To this he barked: 'Too expensive to hear the play-back now; see me at 9.30 in the morning in the cutting room.' Nine a.m. found me in the cutting room. 'Bunny,' I said to the chief recorder, 'let's hear it.' The bell was in the right place. 'What do we do now?' I said. He said: 'You know Ernest as well as I do.' He struck a match and applied it to the roll, which disappeared in a flash. (We had only taken 25 bars.) At 9.30 in stumped E.I. 'Where's that play-back, Bunny?' he said. 'Sorry, guv'nor,' said Bunny, 'there's been a mess-up. The boys thought the tape was a wash-out and have scrapped it.' Ernest passed due judgment on the boys and then said to me: 'I was going to bet you a fiver that you were wrong. We'll call it even: two pound ten apiece to the M.U. Benevolent Fund.'

The tubular bells that are normally used in the orchestra to produce the effect of church bells give the player many uncomfortable moments. A single stroke, recurring strokes, of a peal, such as in the 1812 Overture, can all have their problems. To play the two lengthy chimes required in Berlioz's *Symphonie Fantastique* necessitates the player mounting a raised platform or climbing a ladder. At rehearsal the conductor usually asks to hear the bells. After two strokes the performer is immediately informed, particularly by the members of the orchestra, that the bells are out of tune. To stand behind the row of bells necessary in 1812 is comparable with being behind prison bars. After the first scale one is oblivious of the 'outside world' and utterly reliant on a cue from a member of the percussion squad, or the conductor's beat (if he is visible through the cracks), as to when to 'dry up'.

Such is life behind the drums. Exciting moments intermingled with peaceful ones, such as listening to the second movement of a symphony or one of the Classical piano concertos where the drums are so often *tacet*, or for that matter an aria in a Mozart opera.

Opera has always fascinated me, and I rarely refused an offer of deputising or playing as an extra at Covent Garden where I often played in the stage band, thereby having the privilege of enjoying the bulk of operatic repertoire at close quarters and getting paid for it!

Chamber opera and chamber orchestras have taken a good deal of my time in the last twenty years. As a member of the English Chamber Orchestra, the English Opera Group and the Melos Ensemble, I have taken part in the premières of many of Britten's works—most of which demand much from the percussionist. Britten, however, is engagingly disarming. On one occasion, when presenting me with quite an involved drum part, he said: 'I know it will work, I tried the difficult passages on the table!' Britten's skill in culling the essence from percussion is especially evident in such works as *The Turn of the Screw, Nocturne for Tenor Solo*, the *War Requiem*, and his recent parable operas: *Curlew River, The Burning Fiery Furnace* and *Prodigal Son*. For each of the parable operas he enlisted my co-operation in creating percussion instruments to yield the novel sounds he had in mind. For the final opera of the trilogy he asked for an instrument, possibly a gourd, to give the effect of plodding feet on a monotonous journey. After due experiment I submitted a gourd, partly filled with small shot, which gave (I felt) the required shuffle. 'Let's consider it over lunch,' B.B. said. 'What I really had in mind was a left and a right foot.' With a gourd, conical in shape, the desired effect was produced. One treasures such moments as these, and such stimulating experiences as playing that 'pearl' of percussion, Stravinsky's *Soldier's Tale*, under the composer, or being directed by Walton in a performance of his *Façade*. In contrast one clearly remembers the mortifying experiences of having played immoderately; as I fear I did on a recent Tuesday Invitation Concert. More cherished moments I trust will survive with me, such as wielding the cymbals at the Coronation 1953, under the batons of Sir Adrian Boult and Sir William McKie, and the invitation from Sir Thomas Armstrong to join the professorial staff of the Royal Academy of Music. To which could be added the thrill of seeing a number of my former students behind the drums in some of our most famous orchestras. Equally gratifying could be the high compliment paid to me by a small schoolboy at the conclusion of one of my lecture-recitals, when he assured me that in his opinion I was 'nearly as good as Ringo'!

To conclude, a word of advice. If you have a young friend who has ideas about becoming a percussionist, arrange that he takes $3\frac{1}{2}$ cwt of percussion equipment to a small studio in Soho (where parking is prohibited). After a series of minor incidents he will eventually have the privilege of struggling up three flights of narrow stairs, and the pleasure of assembling (and repairing) his instruments in a dim light. For three hours he will be told, politely or otherwise, that everything he does is below par. At the end of the session he will be obliged to engage in the usual quarrel over porterage rates, after which—thoroughly disillusioned—he will return to street level to find that his vehicle has been towed away by the police. The caretaker of the building will inform him that as it is Friday evening he must get his instruments out immediately, otherwise they will remain there until Monday morning. This necessitates a hired car, the cost of which, coupled with the police fine, amounts to the fee. Such is life with the man behind the drums.

James Blades's book on PERCUSSION INSTRUMENTS AND THEIR HISTORY *has just been published.*

Engraving from Johann Christoph Weigel's *Musicalisches Theatrum*

The Curious Art of Topiary

BY OLIVE COOK
PHOTOGRAPHS BY EDWIN SMITH

ANYONE PASSING along the road between the villages of Budlake and Broadclyst in Devon, except possibly the motorist flashing by at sixty miles an hour, will be struck by an extraordinary image, a giant cock in clipped yew, half filling a tiny cottage garden. Unlike the plaster storks and gnomes of suburbia, this massive rotund bird, with his powerfully curving comb and thick tail, is no gaudy, pertly detailed intruder among the flowers and ferns; he is at one with his roosting place, of the same living green as the little enclosure, imparting to it that magical quality which the Elizabethans called 'faerie' and at the same time giving it a modest claim to rank as a work of art.

This cock would have looked equally at home in the garden of the Tuscan villa described by Pliny the Younger where the space in front of the portico was embellished with box trees cut into the figures of birds and animals, while the ground between them was covered with the flat reliefs of verdant creatures and geometrical devices. Medieval illuminations, such as those of the Harleian *Romaunt of the Rose*, show small trees cut into abstract shapes and tiers, as well as dense, clipped hedges shutting off the formal plot from the wild outside world. And Gervase Markham, writing in 1614, describes the 'knot' or square bed, filled with a design of close-cut box or aromatic herbs, as one of the most ancient of all English garden ornaments. The art of topiary has therefore a long tradition. But it was not until the sixteenth and seventeenth centuries that it reached its zenith.

Different aspects of the art were then emphasised in different parts of Europe. In Italy, especially in Tuscany, it was the architectural character of the tall hedge of shorn yew which appealed to the gardener. Immense walls of sombre green enhanced the symmetry of the layout, encompassed secret gardens and *boscos*, plunged the long, straight alley into romantic shade and threw marble statues and fountains into dazzling relief. But the most spectacularly architectural form of Italian topiary was the *teatro di verdura*, and the most captivating of these green theatres is surely that of the Villa Marlia Fraga near Lucca, where auditorium, wings, conductor's platform and prompter's box have all been shaped in yew while, frozen into stone, the white figures of Harlequin, Columbine and Pantaloon half emerge from umbrageous niches on to the silent, sunlit stage of grass.

French topiarists cultivated above all the knot garden, and developed it into the magnificent parterres of the Renaissance period. At Villandry twelve whole acres of intricate geometric box design, arranged in four tiers, overwhelm the spectator with the sheer extent of their polished artificiality. At Vaux-le-Vicomte nature is yet more fantastically chastened and transformed in a vast spread of flamboyant scrolls below the terrace, viridian ornament on a ground of pink, powdered brick; while at Courance the intimidating formality of the French conception is lightened and animated by a ravishing contrast: the bold swirling patterns of two immense carpets of box are juxtaposed to the glassy sheen of a precisely rectangular lake.

The English contemporaries of these French and Italian topiarists excelled in quite another branch of the art, that of figure sculpture. Barnaby Googe, in his *Husbandry* of 1578, recommends topiary as a suitable pastime for women, who could plant hedges, 'for their pleasure, to grow in sundry proportions and in the fashion of a cart, a peacock or such things as they fancy'. And Markham speaks of hedges simulating battlements which support the leafy figures of beasts, birds, 'creeping things and shippes'. William Lawson, author of *A New Orchard and Garden* (1618), tells of yews in the 'shape of men armed in the field, ready to give battell; or swift running Greyhounds; or of well scented and true running Hounds to chase the Deere or hunt the Hare'. Bacon's garden was surrounded by a hedge decorated with clipped turrets and figures.

The Curious Art of Topiary

Fortunately our knowledge of such collections of living sculpture does not only come from written descriptions: there is an astonishing seventeenth-century survival at Levens Hall, Westmorland. This garden makes a more staggering impact and stirs the imagination more than all the grand conceits of Italy and France, particularly if seen from one of the upper casements of the old stone house. From here the solid green monstrous shapes seem to be advancing on the Hall in lurching, close-set ranks. In the misty English air they appear more strange, more wholly illogical than any of the images seen by Poliphilus in his dream of an enchanted garden on the island of Cythera, and more arbitrarily proportioned than anything encountered by Alice. Giant hats, corkscrews, umbrellas, balls, birds, mammoth sets of weights, and abstract forms pierced by the holes we are apt to regard as peculiar to modern sculpture—more than a hundred pieces crowd a walled court, their dark mass and startling scale intensified by a soft background of deciduous trees.

By the time of William and Mary the English enthusiasm for fantasy, fanned by the Dutch fashion for oddly cut trees, had degenerated into a national mania for wildly extravagant topiary. At Staunton Harold an entire menagerie in yew pranced along the sides of a hollow; London gardens, according to Peter Collinson, were remarkable for 'their clipt yews in the shape of birds, dogs, men, ships, etc.', the bizarre collection of a Mr Parkinson of Lambeth exciting special notice; and several of Kip's views of country seats show rashes of cocks, hens, fans, plumes, discs and balls in yew and box.

This exaggerated craze for topiary was inevitably followed by a reaction against the whole art, which found an able protagonist in Alexander Pope. On Tuesday, September 29, 1713, he published a sarcastic article in *The Guardian* ridiculing the fashion for evergreen imagery:

> For the benefit of all my loving Countrymen of this curious Taste, I shall here publish a Catalogue of Greens to be disposed of by an eminent Town-Gardener who has lately applied to me on this Head.... My Correspondent is arrived to such Perfection that he cuts Family Pieces of Men,

Women and Children. Any Ladies that please may have their own Effigies in Myrtle or their Husbands in Hornbeam. . . . I shall proceed to his Catalogue, as he sent it for my Recommendation.

Adam and *Eve* in Yew; *Adam* a little shattered by the fall of the Tree of Knowledge in the great Storm; *Eve* and the *Serpent* very flourishing. The Tower of *Babel*, not yet finished. *St George* in Box; his Arm scarce long enough but will be in a condition to stick the Dragon by next *April*. A green *Dragon* of the same, with a Tail of Ground Ivy for the present. N.B. *These two are not to be sold separately.*

Edward the *Black Prince* in Cypress. *Laurustine* Bear in Blossom, with a Juniper Hunter in Berries. A Pair of Giants *stunted*, to be sold cheap. A *Queen Elizabeth*, in Phylyrea, a little inclining to Green sickness but of full growth. Another *Queen Elizabeth* in Myrtle, which was very forward, but Miscarried by being too near a Savine. An old Maid of Honour in Wormwood. A topping *Ben Johnson* in Lawrel. Divers eminent Modern Poets in Bays, somewhat blighted, to be disposed of a Pennyworth. A Quick-set Hog shot up into a Porcupine, by its being forgot a week in rainy Weather. A Lavender Pigg with Sage growing in his Belly. *Noah's Ark* in Holly, standing on the Mount; the Ribs a little damaged for want of Water. A Pair of *Maidenheads* in Firr, in great forwardness.

Topiary, together with the formal avenue and the symmetrical layout, was about to be swept away by the landscape school of gardening and the taste for the 'natural' manner. Apart from the evergreen sculpture of Levens and the glorious array at Packwood of huge green monoliths symbolising the Sermon on the Mount, early topiary arrangements have survived the hand of the improver only in fragments. Such are the enchanting doves at Risley Hall, Derbyshire, billing each other to form an archway in a yew hedge, or the colossal, shaggy peacocks casting their great shadows across the tangled moat and sloping lawns of Tudor Kirtling in Cambridgeshire.

For the most part the English topiary tradition lives on only in the country cottage garden, which was untouched by the cult of the picturesque. In view of the rapid decay during the last thirty years of all rural crafts it is surprising how many yew and box sculptures are still skilfully maintained by cottage dwellers. In the course of a single excursion I came upon smooth hedges, thick and formidable as castle walls, scalloped, battlemented and adorned with birds and beasts; cocks crowing from the tops of ringed pillars, cones with button finials, a sitting pheasant, numbers of immense balls, a teapot on a rounded plinth and an impressive cross, as lofty as the wall against which it pressed.

There have been several notable attempts in our own century to revive the art on a grander scale. Topiary plays an important part at Hidcote Manor, for instance, planted some sixty years ago by Lawrence Johnston, though there the small, secret, hedged 'rooms', the green theatre, the marvellous yew pediment and the rows of smooth pinnacles are Italian in inspiration. The yew chessmen in their formal setting in front of the little Norman manor of Hemingford are closer to our native tradition. But the most imaginative and the most truly English of all twentieth-century topiary gardens is that at Great Dixter, planned by Nathaniel Lloyd. Here gargantuan coffee pots, fighting cocks measuring six feet from beak to tail, a crow-stepped arch, peacocks perching unsteadily on voluminous pyramids and ponderous domes, grow in that timeless domain of sliding scale, of smooth, dark solidity, of bewitching stillness which is the peculiar creation of the master sculptor in evergreen.

In a manual on the methods of planting and cultivating yew and box, published in 1925, Nathaniel Lloyd encouragingly dismisses as a popular fallacy the belief that yew is slow of growth. Yet photographs of a shaped tree in his own garden taken at different stages of its development show that the desired form was only fully realised after some fifteen years. The 'twenties already belong wholly to the past. Who in this speed-obsessed and mortgage-minded world of the late 'sixties would plant for a more distant future than four or five years? Until some sense of stability and security is restored, there is as little prospect for the delightful and extraordinary art of topiary as for civilisation itself.

Cock in yew in a cottage garden near Broadclyst, Devon

The figure of Columbine in the Teatro di Verdura, Villa Marlia Fraga, near Lucca, Italy

The box parterre on its gravel background at Courance, Seine-et-Oise, France

On the right: clipped box and yew at Levens Hall, Westmorland. This unique topiary garden is said to have been laid out by the 'Monsieur Beaumont', gardener to King James II, whose portrait hangs on the staircase wall at Levens. It is more likely that the Frenchman's work at Levens consisted in the planting of the fine beech *allées* in the Continental style; and that the typically English topiary is earlier in date.

Above: another view of Levens showing the contrast between the solid topiary forms and the background of deciduous trees. On the left: A cross in yew at Chipping Campden, Gloucestershire

At the top, on the right: cocks surmounting tiered columns in yew, at Sapperton, Gloucestershire.
Below, on the right: privet hedges at Amersham, Buckinghamshire.

Two aspects of the topiary garden at Great Dixter, Sussex, planted by Nathaniel Lloyd, an authority on yew, during the first quarter of the present century.

On the right: yew hedge and cock at Amersham, Buckinghamshire.
Below: hedges and pediment of mixed foliage at Hidcote Manor, Gloucestershire, planted by Lawrence Johnston since 1907.

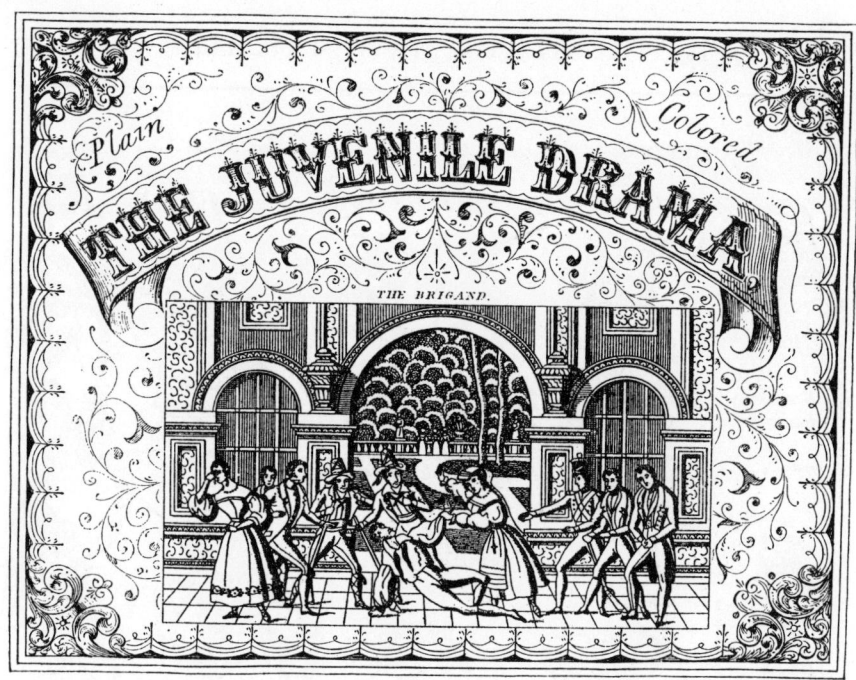

The Brigand in the Toy Theatre

BY GEORGE SPEAIGHT

THE ENGLISH TOY THEATRE was a toy and a theatre and a form of popular art. As a toy it has provided a creative plaything for generations of children, mostly boys, ever since it was invented in 1811; the sheets of small characters were coloured, mounted on cardboard, and cut out; the scenery was placed in position on a model stage; the characters were clipped into slides and pushed on; the curtain was rolled up and the play was performed. As a theatre it has preserved in miniature a whole corpus of the drama of the Regency and early Victorian

The Brigand Chief reposing and the Dying Brigand. Engravings from the paintings by Charles Eastlake (Dodie Masterman Collection)

The Brigand in the Toy Theatre

period; about three hundred plays were adapted for toy theatre performance during the fifty or so years during which it flourished, and every one of these plays was originally produced upon the human stage. As a form of popular art, published by a hundred theatrical printsellers, it enshrines a particular kind of unsophisticated vision, a particular school of journeyman engraving, and a particular technique of rapid hand-colouring—'twopence coloured'—that has given a phrase to the language.

All this has been said often enough, but it might be interesting to see just how it applies to any given example. Let us pick up some toy theatre sheets, almost at random. 'Pollock's characters and scenes in The Brigand' were on sale up to a few years ago at Benjamin Pollock's toy theatre shop for a few shillings—seven plates of characters, seven scenes and three plates of wings, with a playbook. Well within living memory they could have been bought at old Mr Pollock's shop in Hoxton Street for the original price of a penny a sheet plain or twopence coloured. *The Brigand* is a romantic drama, complicated at the best of times and almost incomprehensible in a synopsis; but here is a sketch of the bare bones of the plot.

Massaroni is the chief of a band of brigands who gain a living by plundering travellers on the roads in and out of Rome. His principal enemy is the Governor of Rome, Prince Bianchi, who sends his troops on a series of ineffectual forays to destroy the band. Two students of the French Academy, Albert and Theodore, are captured by the brigands while sketching some Roman antiquities and are held for ransom. They ask to be allowed to return to their home to raise the ransom money, and the staccato dialogue, which is one of the charms of the toy theatre, continues:

MASSARONI What security have I that you will keep your word?
ALBERT I swear by the holy cross upon your breast, to send the sum on demand before midnight.
MASSARONI Your name?
ALBERT Albert Deschamps.
MASSARONI You are free.
THEODORE You don't say so?
MASSARONI Away to our retreat in the mountains.

In the retreat in the mountains a member of the band announces, 'Female peasants are ascending the mountains with provisions,' and a gay dance of brigands and peasants takes place until it is interrupted by the sentry warning, 'A carriage winds round the road at the foot of the mountain.' A stage direction instructs that 'The sound of wheels is heard without' and Massaroni declares, 'There's gold in the sound! Load, comrades! And descend the mountain in silence.'

The second act opens in Prince Bianchi's palace in Rome, where the French students are attending a reception. An unexpected guest, the Count de Strozzi, is announced, and turns out to be none other than Massaroni in disguise come to collect the ransom in person. He hoodwinks the Governor, chatting about the brigands of the district, and the Governor boastfully declares that he intends to put a stop to Massaroni's depredations:

The Brigand in the Toy Theatre

PRINCE BIANCHI I intend—
MASSARONI (aside) This may be worth hearing. (aloud) You intend to—
PRINCE BIANCHI Yes: I intend to take him tonight if possible. For I know where to lay my hand upon him at this moment.
MASSARONI Indeed! He may escape your Highness.
PRINCE BIANCHI Impossible! I mean to strike a sure blow at once. I must leave you to dispatch the detachment.

But, as the Governor is about to send his troops on a wild-goose chase, Massaroni is recognised by one of the company whom he had robbed only that morning:

MASSARONI Curses on the old steward of St Arnulph! I am discovered! I cannot escape!—I have a brace of pistols and a dagger about me! I will sell my life dearly!

In an extraordinary mêlée the French students try to aid Massaroni's escape, he sees a portrait in the palace which he recognises as that of his mother, sliding panels open and close, soldiers open fire, the portrait is identified as that of a peasant girl once loved but abandoned by the Prince, Massaroni is fatally wounded, the identity of his mother is disclosed, and as he dies the Prince cries: 'My son, my son!'

Let us follow back the development of these charming and unpretentious sheets of characters and scenes. Pollock first published them in about 1876, but before that they had been issued in identically the same form by his father-in-law, John Redington, in about 1850. Redington, in his turn, had acquired the plates from a publisher called J. K. Green, who had first issued this play in 1836. Another version which seems to have copied the arrangement of Green's characters was also published at about this time by the firm of Skelt—later to be immortalised by Robert Louis Stevenson in his famous essay on the toy theatre. Green had created his version of the play by combining a selection of characters that his artist had copied, more or less distantly, from the editions previously published by Dyer and West. William West was perhaps the earliest and certainly the most accomplished publisher of toy theatre plays—or the Juvenile Drama, as it was called; his sheets for *The Brigand*, which are

[continued on page 213]

Scene 2.
POLLOCK'S SCENES IN THE BRIGAND.
No. 3.
London. Published by B. Pollock, 73 Hoxton Street, Hoxton.

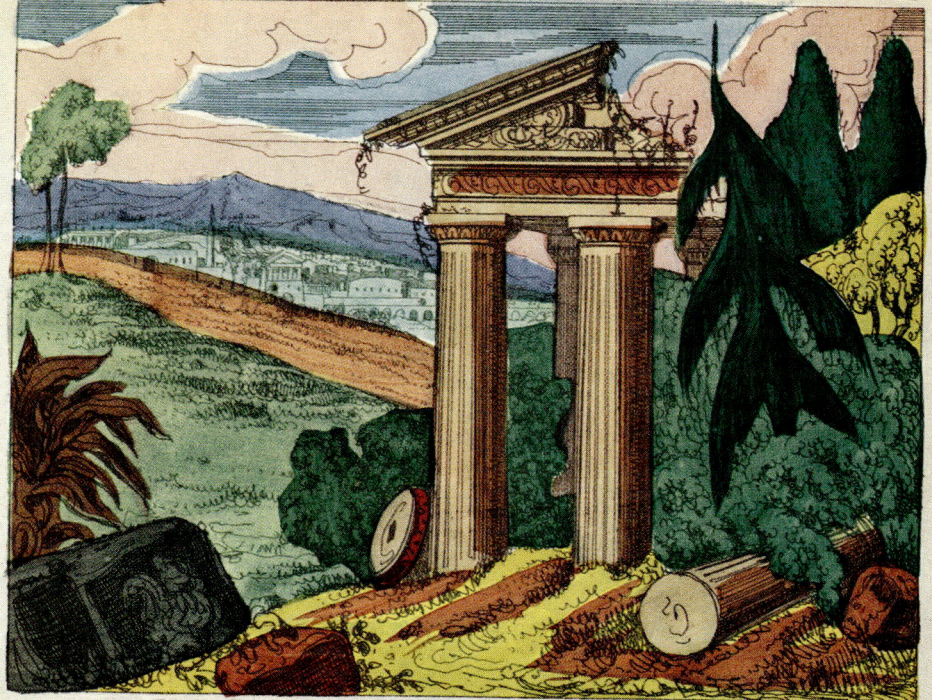

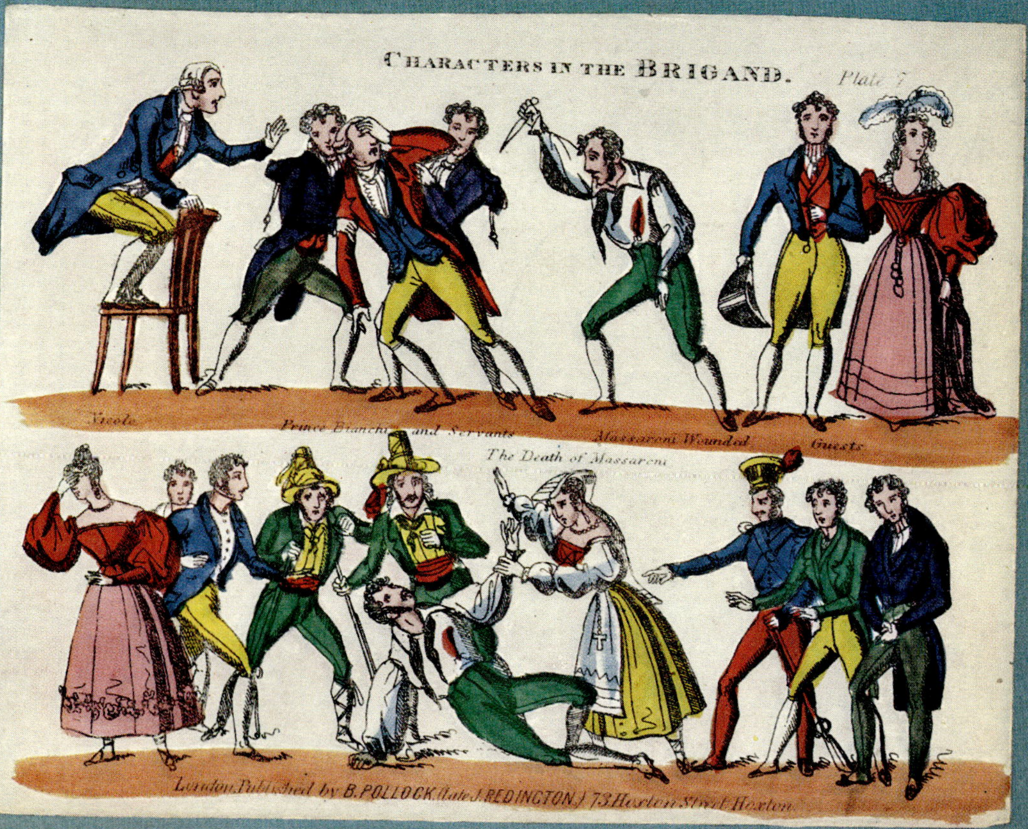
CHARACTERS IN THE BRIGAND.
Plate 7
Nicolo
Prince Bianchi and Servants
Massaroni Wounded
Guests
The Death of Massaroni
London. Published by B. POLLOCK (late J. REDINGTON) 73 Hoxton Street Hoxton.

Back of Scene 6   POLLOCK'S SCENES IN THE BRIGAND.   N.º 7.

London, Published by B. Pollock, 73, Hoxton Street, Hoxton.

Above: the Brigand Chief's wife clings to the edge of a cliff as she anxiously watches the battle below. An engraving from the painting by Charles Eastlake. Compare the toy theatre treatment of this incident in Pollock's sheet of characters, plate 2 (author's Collection).
Opposite: a toy theatre scene of the outskirts of Rome (below) and the view of Naples from which it was copied (above) (Dodie Masterman Collection).

POLLOCK'S CHARACTERS & SCENES IN THE BRIGAND.

7 Plates Characters, 7 Scenes.
3 Plates Wings Nº 9,10,13.

A Book Written for the Above Price 4ᵈ

Massaroni.   Maria Grazie.

Brigand.   Rubaldi.   Massaroni & Maria Grazie.   Brigand.

London Published by B. Pollock, 73, Hoxton Street, Hoxton.

POLLOCK'S CHARACTERS IN THE BRIGAND.   Plate 2.

Brigand.   Nicolo.   Massaroni 2ᵈ dress.   Massaroni.   Maria Grazie.

Theodore.   Albert.   Massaroni.   Maria Grazie.   Massaroni.

London Published by B. Pollock, 73, Hoxton Street, Hoxton.

really exquisite engravings and the last play he published, were issued in 1831.

West drew his play from the living theatre. *The Brigand* had been written by James Robinson Planché and had been first performed at Drury Lane in 1829, with the melodramatic favourite, James Wallack, in the title rôle. Planché was a fascinating character, a prolific dramatist responsible for innumerable melodramas, opera libretti, extravaganzas, burlesques and pantomimes, a gifted musician, an antiquarian, a Fellow of the Society of Antiquaries, the author of a scholarly history of costume, and an authority on heraldry who became Rouge Croix Pursuivant of Arms and later Somerset Herald.

And where did Planché get his idea for *The Brigand* from? The basic plot seems to have come from the French, perhaps from Gilbert de Pixerécourt, but there was another—a pictorial—source. 'In this melodrama', he tells us in his *Recollections and Reflections*, 'I introduced three tableaux from Eastlake's well-known pictures, "An Italian Brigand Chief reposing", "The Wife of a Brigand Chief watching the result of a Battle", and "The Dying Brigand", engravings of which had been just published ... and were in all the print-shop windows. They were very effective.'

Charles Eastlake had gone to Italy in 1817, 'one of the first English artists to visit Rome after the peace', we are told in *The Imperial Dictionary of Universal Biography*: after a short stay in Greece he returned to Italy, and 'from this time he took up his residence at Rome for many years and painted a series of characteristic pictures from the life of the Greek and Italian peasantry ... his favourite pictures, however, were banditti scenes'. Eastlake went on to become Sir Charles, Director of the National Gallery, and President of the Royal Academy. His autobiography relates how he was furnished with the authentic costume and accoutrements of a real brigand of the Abruzzi during his residence in Rome.

It is a far cry from the budding P.R.A., scanning the artist's models on the Spanish Steps and painting them against picturesque landscapes of the Alban Hills, in the 1820s, to a handful of toy theatre sheets, lying in a toyshop window in the Hoxton slums in the 1920s. But the same theme—the Brigand Chief reposing, the Brigand's wife watching, and the Dying Brigand—forms a link to unite them. Introduced as tableaux into a Drury Lane spectacular, copied and recopied by a succession of piratical printsellers, printed in reverse and transformed almost out of recognition, the composition of Eastlake's canvases may still be discerned even in the crudest of the toy theatre versions.

The scenery, like the characters, was copied from the real theatre. Though the original sets have disappeared, we may feel tolerably certain that the toy theatre *décor* bears at least a general resemblance to that of the Drury Lane production of 1829. But one scene presented a difficulty to the toy theatre artist: the final scene depicts an apartment in the villa of Prince Bianchi, on the outskirts of Rome; 'the folding doors at back to be made to open, and scene 7 to be put at back, so as to be seen through the folding doors', the toy theatre stage directions inform us. (An impression of the effect achieved can be seen in the engraving on the play-packet cover reproduced at the head of this article). It is clear that the audience could catch only a partial glimpse of the back scene, no. 7, and the toy theatre artist attending the performance would have been unable to copy the full extent of a backcloth from what he saw through the folding doors. What was to be done? He might, of course, have invented a design for himself; but the toy theatre artists were not normally originators of any distinction, and yet scene 7 in the Green-Redington-Pollock version is a particularly charming composition.

The mystery of the origin of scene 7 was recently solved by a felicitous chance when Mrs Dodie Masterman, an amateur of toy theatre art with an exceptionally acute eye for its singularities of draughtsmanship and engraving, was passing through one of the antique supermarkets that have sprung up in recent years to the delight of the London pedestrian. She suddenly spied, hanging in one of the stalls, an engraving of a 'Distant View of Naples' that seemed familiar. With a whoop of discovery she bore it home. It was indeed the origin of Pollock's scene 7! The toy theatre artist possessed sufficient knowledge of geography to omit the distant sea, but in all other respects a faithful copy of a view towards the Bay of Naples has become a very adequate panorama of Rome from the Pincio. Further research has established the date of the Naples engraving as about 1828, which places it in its logical chronological position in relation to the Green publication of 1836.

These few characters and scenes for Pollock's *The Brigand*, therefore, carry curious and unexpected links with more pretentious forms of art. In these toy theatre sheets, frozen in sleep as if in the palace of the Sleeping Beauty, the romantic vision of a Regency artist lives on; in these toy theatre sheets nineteenth-century actors spring to life again with their histrionic gestures; in these toy theatre sheets the scenery of early Victorian stages glows once more. The toy theatre is, indeed, a reversed telescope, of time rather than optics, through which we may look at the theatre and the art of Regency and early Victorian England, and find it there, in miniature, miraculously, alive.

A new edition of George Speaight's THE TOY THEATRE *has recently been published*

Rubaldo   Massaroni asleep   Maria Grazie

Joys of the Jigsaw
BY LINDA HANNAS

A PICTURE mounted on board and cut into irregular pieces—that is the modern definition of a jigsaw puzzle. Fifty or even a hundred and fifty years ago the same description would have made sense. But the name wouldn't. Until this century they were known to children as Dissected Puzzles. That great propounder of educational theories, Richard Lovell Edgeworth, used them freely for his own prodigious family. 'They are favourites', he said, 'because they require ingenuity and address in putting together and'; he added, 'because they fill up a considerable portion of time'. The kind of family that Jane Austen knew and wrote about used them. Poor Fanny Price, in *Mansfield Park*, was much derided by her more wealthy cousins when she went to stay with them. 'Just think, Mama, she is unable to put the map of Europe together.'

But when were these puzzles first made? By whom? And why?

In the 1760s a cartographer and printseller, later to become drawing master at Harrow School, was trading from Russell Court, Drury Lane. He hit on the ingenious idea of mounting some of his maps on wood, cutting them up into pieces and selling them in boxes to be reassembled. His entry in a London street directory for 1763 reads:

> Spilsbury, John, Engraver and Map Dissector in Wood,
> in order to facilitate the Teaching of Geography,
> Russell-court, Drury-lane.

Here, more than two hundred years ago, was the inventor of jigsaws, and here too was their *raison d'être*. They were no mere toys like the cheap puzzles on sale today—expendable as plastic cups. They were designed specifically to teach, and were intended to last.

John Spilsbury advertised some thirty different dissected maps. His prices, which ranged from seven and sixpence to one guinea, must have put them into the luxury class in those days. These maps were finely engraved, hand-coloured and carefully cut along the boundaries of counties or countries. They were mounted on mahogany and sold either in custom-made rectangular oak boxes, or, more cheaply, in oval chip boxes. Some maps could be had for a further saving of four and sixpence, 'without the sea'.

Looking back from our cornucopian age of toys, when jigsaw puzzles cover such a multitude of subjects, it is difficult to believe that for the first twenty years or so maps were the only subjects to be dissected. The breakthrough came in 1787, with a puzzle consisting of medallion portraits of the thirty-two monarchs, from William I to George II, arranged in their chronological order. Each monarch was surrounded by the relevant dates, dynasty and notable events of his reign. And each was cut into a similar sized but wavy-edged rectangle, which made the puzzle extremely difficult to assemble without knowing the order of the kings. It was called, *Engravings for Teaching the Elements of English History and Chronology after the Manner of Dissected Maps for Teaching Geography*. Directions printed on the puzzle advised:

1. Learn to put the heads together in succession. 2. Get the dates and the houses of the respective kings. 3. Learn the names of the principal personages separately. 4. Get by heart the chronological and historical facts of the respective reigns, with the dates of battles, treaties, etc.

One of the publishers of this puzzle, William Darton, a quaker, then at Birchin Lane, London, was the founder of a notable family business which published children's books, games and dissected puzzles over a period of about sixty years. Curiously, having instigated the historical puzzle, Darton seems to have turned his back on English history as a subject, not using it again until 1815. It was left to his rival in the children's games business, John Wallis, another founder of a family firm, to popularise the historical puzzle.

Wallis was quick to see the potentials of combining the teaching of history with play. A year later, in 1788, he published a far less onerous puzzle along the same lines—*Chronological*

Tables of English History for the Instruction of Youth. But he cut down heavily on the information surrounding each monarch and he printed no directions on the puzzle about imbibing the knowledge. He seems to have struck exactly the right balance between medicine and sugar. If any conclusion can be drawn from the extreme rarity of the Darton puzzle and the comparative abundance of the Wallis one of just a year later, it is that the former was a failure, with only a few copies sold, and the latter a fantastic success. Indeed Wallis re-issued his *Chronological Tables* in its original form in 1799—eleven years later.

Hard on the heels of historical puzzles came another *genre*. More manufacturers were coming into the field; there was a limit to the number of maps and historical tables which could be sold; but the climate in children's recreation was still strongly didactic.

The teaching of religion and moral behaviour was already firmly established as an integral part of children's literature and sheet games of the period, and so it was a natural step to incorporate it into dissected puzzles. And it had a conveniently wide range. As well as including biblical history—the source of splendidly graphic material—it could embrace such diverse writers as Benjamin Franklin and John Bunyan.

Wallis seized on both these authors. In 1790 he issued a hand-coloured engraving of *The Pilgrim's Progress Dissected*, showing the path which Christian took on his journey from the City of Destruction, at the bottom of the puzzle, to the Holy Land, at the top. It was designed, he said, as a Rational Amusement for Youth of Both Sexes. And the following year he issued an ingenious rebus puzzle based on the writings of Benjamin Franklin. When the puzzle was completed the child could set about deciphering the curious arrangement of pictures and letters. In this the moneyless were informed 'how they can reinforce their purses ... and how to keep them always full. Two simple rules well observed, will do the business. 1st, Let honesty and toil be thy constant companion. 2nd, Spend one penny every day, less than thy clear gains.'

Benjamin Franklin was used by another publisher too— Bowles and Carver. In 1795 they issued a fine engraving by Robert

Dighton, caricaturist and portrait painter, called *Bowles's Moral Pictures; or Poor Richard Illustrated. Being Lessons for the Young and the Old, on Industry, Temperance, Frugality &c.* In it strictures like, 'Want of care does more damage than want of knowledge,' and 'By diligence and perseverance the mouse eat the cable in two,' were illustrated.

By the end of the first decade of the nineteenth century a welcome change was well under way. The old, harsh moral teaching of the eighteenth century was taking on a kindlier form and the tone of the puzzles was softening. And once again this was following the trend in children's literature.

That delightful family, the Taylors of Ongar—of whom the most famous were Ann and Jane— had brought a new gentleness into the nurseries with their verse for children. One poem which has become part of children's lore is 'Twinkle, twinkle little star'. This was first printed in 1806, but two years earlier they had written *Original Poems for Infant Minds*. This was published by the Darton family and was so successful that a new edition appeared every year until 1834. One of the poems from this collection which was often published singly, and usually without permission, was 'My Mother'. It is hardly surprising then that Darton should use this, and the inevitable imitations which followed, for jigsaws. In 1811 *My Mother* appeared—beautifully engraved and coloured, six pictures illustrating the twelve verses.

> When pain and sickness made me cry,
> Who gaz'd upon my heavy eye,
> And wept for fear that I should die?
> My Mother.

This was followed next year by *My Grandmother* and *My Bible*.

> Who taught me in my youthful days,
> Ever to walk in wisdom's ways,
> And every day my God to praise?
> My Bible.

It was in this period, some fifty years after Spilsbury had first begun dissecting his maps, that John Wallis claimed to be their inventor. In 1812 he began using engraved labels on his boxes which read:

> J. Wallis the Original Manufacturer of Dissected Maps and Puzzles (having dedicated full 30 Years to that particular line of business) requests the Public to Observe that all his dissected Articles are superior both in correctness & workmanship to any in London ...

This fulsome piece of publicity can best be accounted for by the ever-growing competition in the jigsaw field. But he was a businessman and probably judged that a claim stated was a claim believed. The superiority of his dissections to any in London might have been valid were it not for the excellent puzzles constantly emerging from his old rivals the Dartons, in Holborn Hill. But the claim to have been the *original* manufacturer was patently absurd. He must have reckoned on the old Spilsbury puzzles having been forgotten. Be that as it may, his claim remained unchallenged for a hundred and fifty years, and books on children's toys have all quoted his name as the supposed inventor of jigsaws. Only quite recently have John Spilbury's puzzles, his entry in the London directory and his trade cards been brought out, dusted, and set up to show him as the real original manufacturer of dissected maps.

Towards mid-century, with the decline of both Darton and Wallis, new firms, such as John Betts, began to establish themselves and develop a style of their own. At the same time there were numerous small printers who never put their name on their puzzles. This all made for an interesting diversity of subject matter.

Generally speaking it was the small back-street manufacturer who cashed in on topical events like the Lord Mayor's Show, the Coronation and the Wedding of Queen Victoria. Incidentally, a less happy event prompted a publisher from quite another field to try for some easy money. A. Park, of 47 Leonard Street, Finsbury, usually to be found publishing toy theatre material, produced a dramatic little puzzle out of the abortive attempt on the Queen's life in 1840. But the usual run of anonymous publishers used poor quality wood, and the engraving, colouring

[continued on page 229]

Opposite: *The Pilgrim's Progress Dissected* published in 1790 by J. Wallis,

Above: Bowles's *Moral Pictures; or Poor Richard Illustrated*, published by Bowles & Carver in 1795. Opposite: *The Hill of Science*, published in 1807 by John Wallis, showing the way from the Barren Land of Ignorance, at the bottom, to the Temple of Truth, at the top. Below: a section of *The Cries of London*, published by William Darton.

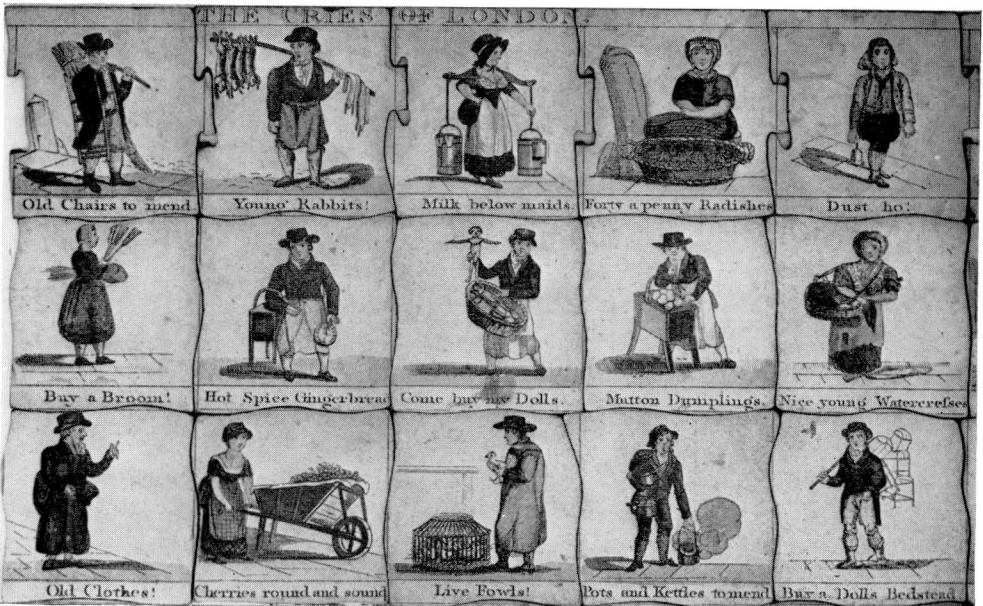

My Bible
by WILLIAM JOLLY.

What taught me in my Youthful days,
Ever to walk in wisdom's ways,
And every day my God to Praise?
  MY BIBLE.

What bade me have an upright heart,
To act through life an honest part,
Nor have recourse to guile or art?
  MY BIBLE.

What told me I should not profane
The Sabbath day, but love the name,
And e'er revere its sacred name?
  MY BIBLE.

What told me I should learn to shun,
Whatever was by Sinners done,
And from the Paths of vice to run?
  MY BIBLE.

What told me ne'er to turn mine eye,
From Widow's tears, or Orphan's cry,
But Pity feel, for mis'ry's sigh?
  MY BIBLE.

What taught me love and peace to bear,
To all Mankind, to act sincere,
As though the eye of God were near?
  MY BIBLE.

What made me shun each evil way,
What made me love at home to stay,
And night and morn, my Prayers to say?
  MY BIBLE.

Then thro' my life may I revere
The sacred Page, still hold it dear,
For 'tis a source of Comfort here.
  MY BIBLE.

Through this were taught, whence goodness sprung
In whose just praise, the valley rung;
"O! let me have" cried every tongue,
  A BIBLE!

What told me I should ever love,
Almighty God who reigns above,
Nor fail each day the same to prove?
  MY BIBLE.

May ignorance no longer reign,
Henceforth the Heathen shall proclaim
His Makers love—and bless the name of
  BIBLE!

And, when old Age shall weaken me,
My constant care on earth shall be,
To live with God and often see
  MY BIBLE.

Above: *Trades and Manufactures*, published by William Spooner about 1843. Opposite: *Robinson Crusoe*, published by James Izzard about 1820–30, and *My Bible*, by William Jolly, published by William Darton, junr., in 1812. Below: part of a *Multiplication Table, Neatly Dissected*, c. 1820.

The box label of *Edward Oxford firing at Her Majesty*, published by A. Park in 1840. The label design is part of the puzzle picture, which extends to the right, showing four horses drawing the carriage.

There is no publisher given for *Railway Scenes*, of which the box label is illustrated above, but it is assumed to be dated about 1850.

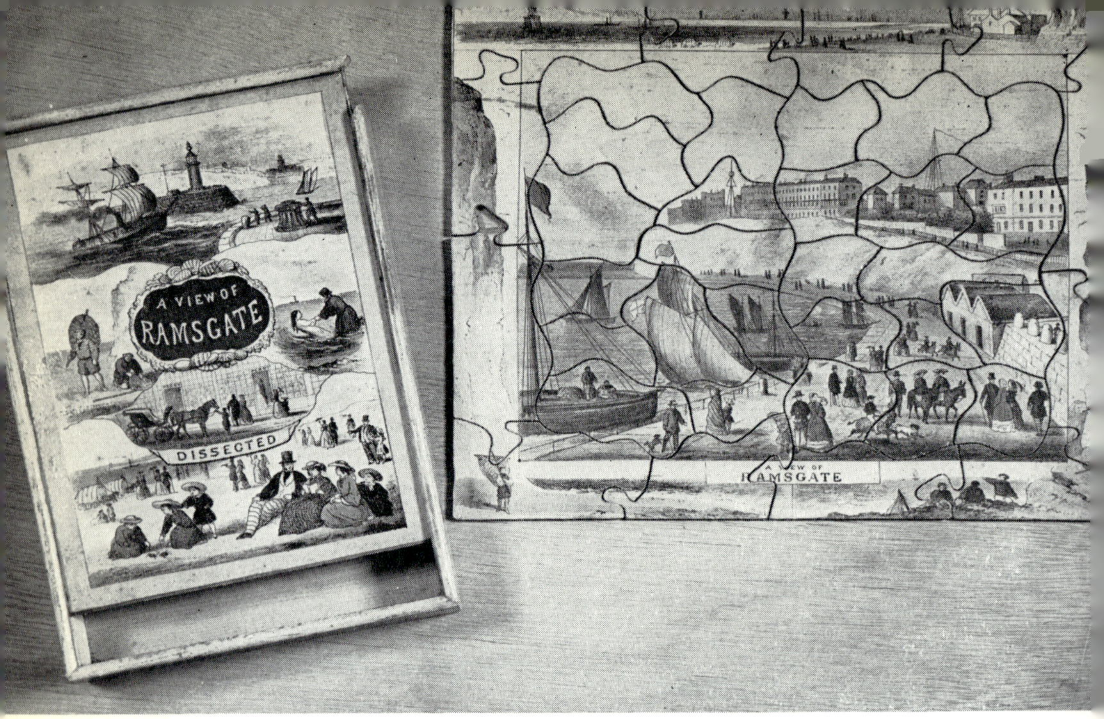
A VIEW OF
RAMSGATE
DISSECTED
A VIEW OF
RAMSGATE

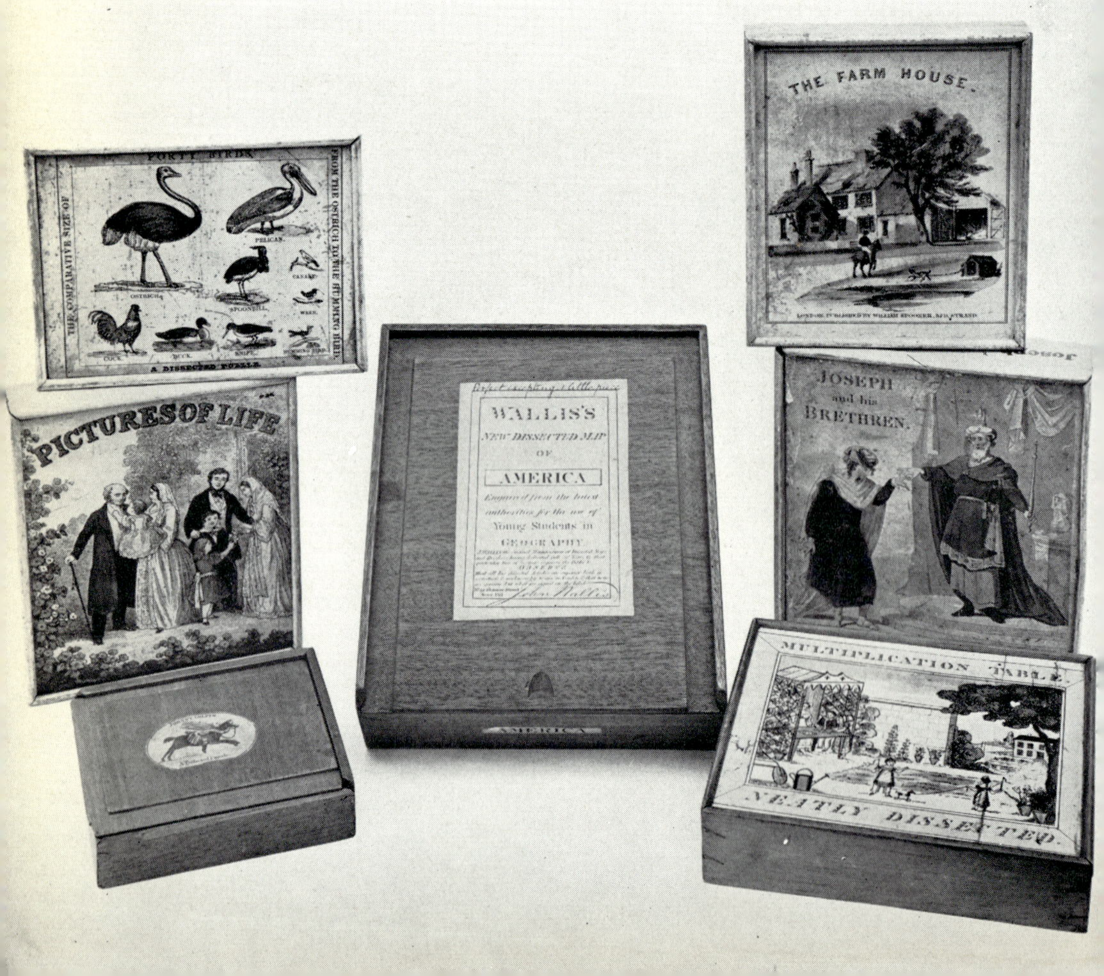
THE FARM HOUSE.
THE COMPARATIVE SIZE OF
FROM THE OSTRICH TO THE HUMMING BIRD
PELICAN
A DISSECTED PUZZLE
PICTURES OF LIFE
WALLIS'S
NEW DISSECTED MAP
OF
AMERICA
Engraved from the latest
authorities for the use of
Young Students in
GEOGRAPHY
AMERICA
JOSEPH
and his
BRETHREN.
MULTIPLICATION TABLE
NEATLY DISSECTED.

and cutting were often crude. They must have been sold cheaply, sometimes perhaps as souvenirs on street corners, but these transient playthings come to us now with a naïve freshness not found in the handsomely produced puzzles from the accredited manufacturers.

However, since there had to be other subjects for puzzles besides topical events, the anonymous band based their subjects to some extent on those of the regular publishers—though with less emphasis on religion, history and geography. Fun was more likely to be found without an imprint.

A mid-nineteenth-century parent thinking back nostalgically to the Wallis and Darton puzzles he had been brought up on would have had some difficulty in finding anything which compared favourably. And for once there might have been some truth in the feeling known to every parent that the toys his child plays with are not as good as his own used to be. Had he, however, been seeking a well-made puzzle, adequately boxed and labelled and usually with a descriptive booklet as well as a key-picture, then he need have looked no further than the ubiquitous John Betts.

From his premises in the Strand, Betts was at that time well under way to establishing his flowing output of table games and dissected puzzles which was to continue until the 1870s. His main lines were bible history and maps—with the odd tangential flip into shipbuilding and even John Gilpin. His work could not really be faulted. It was consistently careful and usually didactic and had the added bonus of the explanatory booklet. But always predictably prosaic.

However, there was one publisher who might have measured up to the nostalgic dreams—William Spooner. In common with most dissected puzzle makers, he was an important publisher of sheet games—those forerunners of Snakes and Ladders and

---

Opposite are shown, with its box label, a very attractive *View of Ramsgate*, published about 1860, and a group of box labels, including that of *Wallis's New Dissected Map of America* and the label of *Multiplication Table Neatly Dissected*, c. 1820, which is of special interest as the earliest picture of children actually assembling a jigsaw.

Joys of the Jigsaw

Monopoly—but his period of puzzle production was little more than ten years. The quality of his work, however, was outstanding. Using hand-coloured lithographs, he chose subjects like *The Hay Field* and *The Farm House*, and treated them in a gently idyllic manner, though always with an eye to interesting, instructive detail. His *History of a Loaf, The Sugar Plantation*, and *Trades and Manufactures* were all designed to catch the imagination of a child—to answer the question 'how?'

Throughout the nineteenth century the teaching of many different subjects was attempted by means of the jigsaw. Multiplication tables were often used, also lessons in spelling, telling the time, and natural history. This last subject ranged from grim rows of stiffly drawn shells 'arranged according to the System of Linnaeus and Dissected as a puzzle' to more pleasingly lighthearted visits to the Zoo. But biblical history, although always present, rose to its peak of popularity in the latter part of the century.

Pictures drawn purely for entertainment, with no didactic overtones at all, were slow to encroach. Dissected puzzles were, after all, designed to facilitate learning. In the eighteenth century fun puzzles were almost unknown; but they made a little headway in the early part of the new century. From the 1850s onwards, however, nursery rhymes became freely used, while seaside scenes, children's parties and other domestic subjects—often very sentimentalised—became popular.

Into this period of crowded market, when manufacturers were vying with each other over diversity of subject and the distinctiveness of their boxes, came one who, with a singlemindedness worthy of Spilsbury, produced only maps. For about fifty years *Superior Dissected Maps, published by Wm. Peacock, London*, were bought for the homes and the classrooms of British children. Many are still around in the Victoriana shops today—and most of these look depressingly little used. Unlike Spilsbury, who engraved his own, Peacock used maps from well-known publishers like George Philip & Son. His own name appeared only on the box label. In complete contrast to the rest of the publishers, these labels of his remained virtually unchanged for about forty years—four female figures representing the continents standing against a background of relevant animals and plants. But with his half-century of publishing Peacock spanned the period during which dissected puzzles slowly changed from being hand-made, highly individualistic playthings to the cheap, mass-produced ones sold in the twentieth century.

During the last decades of the nineteenth century colour printing ousted the hand-coloured engravings, and conformity took over. Before this, each puzzle made from the same engraving had been different—the difference varying in degree. Quality publishers like Darton, Wallis and Spooner varied only slightly. But at the other end of the scale two similar puzzles from one of the smaller and perhaps anonymous firms set side by side may show major differences in colouring. And similarly, with this kind of publishing, great variations occur between the picture on the puzzle and the key-picture. A horse may be brown on the key-picture and grey on the puzzle, and the colour of the rider's clothes might undergo similar changes.

During Peacock's span, too, the change from mahogany to whitewood was finally completed. Until mid-century all puzzles had been mounted on thin boards of mahogany. But whitewood gradually took over. It was cheaper in spite of the fact that, unlike mahogany, it needed a backing of paper to prevent splitting during the cutting. By the time Peacock left the scene, mahogany was a thing of the past.

A similar change, but this time in boxes, occurred before Peacock's time. The earliest boxes, those of Spilsbury and a very few of Wallis's, were of oak. But oak soon gave way to mahogany, and these boxes, beautifully made with sliding lids, remained in fashion until well into the nineteenth century. However, the labels on the mahogany boxes were usually small and unexciting. With the coming of whitewood boxes, labels became a feature. They covered the entire lid. They were brightly pictorial. Indeed one label of about 1820—*Multiplication Tables, Neatly Dissected*— actually provides us with the earliest contemporary picture of children putting together a jigsaw. The labels were hand-coloured and, like the rest of the box, they were varnished. The loss in the quality of the wood was amply made up for by the new gaiety of the box as a whole.

Joys of the Jigsaw

The cutting of puzzles did not change much from the late eighteenth century to the beginning of the current one. Spilsbury's puzzles, and those immediately following his, had no interlocking pieces at all. But by the 1780s both Wallis and Darton were making them with an interlocking border, thus assuring a certain rigidity when it was completed by the child. But such was the difficulty in cutting the small interlocking pieces that this practice of having only the border interlocking continued for well over a hundred years—at any rate in England. Furthermore, by present-day standards the pieces were large, and so, probably more by force of circumstances than anything else, jigsaws remained during this period specifically for children.

Even with the small number of pieces which were used until this century—somewhere between forty and a hundred—no two puzzles were cut alike. It is impossible to fit a piece of one puzzle into another of the same design. Possibly in an attempt to depersonalise the character of the cutter, a few eighteenth-century publishers incorporated cutting lines in the engraving. It was a short-lived experiment and was really in vain. Character still shines through—in evasion of ill-considered curves and incursions into unmarked territory.

Today all the problems are overcome. Jigsaws can be mass-produced cheaply—colour printing takes the place of hand-colouring, cardboard of wood. And diestamping ensures absolute conformity and an all but limitless number of pieces. How would Spilsbury, Darton or Wallis react to a four-thousand-piece, fully interlocking, wavy-edged adult puzzle? As the ultimate in dissections? Or, a monstrous waste of time?

All the jigsaw puzzles illustrated are from the collection of Mrs Linda Hannas.

Making a Pot
BY TONY BIRKS

THERE IS NOTHING quite as effective as clay for creating domestic chaos. It gets trodden into carpets, embedded into cufflinks and the settings of engagement rings; a fine powdery dust spreads everywhere; and wet hands, wrapped around door handles, leave marks which are, I suppose, easier to clean than the U-bends of domestic sinks, blocked with depressing regularity. Pottery clay is much worse than wood shavings, or embroidery satins, or rug wools, for making a mess; and clothes and towels, natural targets for sticky hands, suffer most of all. It must be the creative potential of a lump of soft clay which draws so many people with differing degrees of skill to bear bravely the worn-down fingernails and aching arms for the special satisfaction of making a pot.

I often wonder idly who it was that first grasped the usefulness, the significance, of baking clay by fire. I expect it was a spontaneous, collective discovery, like the 'brainwave' of setting fire to a piece of black coal, the delightful bonus of a chance contiguity. But there is a ritual significance in the firing process which separates the act of making from the finished article. One cannot open the door when the pots are firing, as one can when food is cooking. In a factory which is making plates and cups the kiln is just part of an inevitable routine, but for a potter using his hands and mind to make an expressive gesture, surrendering the pot he has finished to the kiln is an exciting, anxious time. Even a modern sculptor using an oxy-acetylene lamp has a more direct control over what he is doing, and he has the opportunity of changing his mind. Inside the kiln the potter's work will shrink, bend, even explode, scattering fragments which may bring down the whole kiln load like a pack of cards. Later, when the pots are glazed, the dull grey or pink powder on the surface of the clay is magically transformed into a vibrant rich colour after the fire, but when it is all happening, all that the potter can do is to peer with shaded eyes through the spy-hole in the kiln wall, where everything is white, and an even more brilliant halo outlines the profiles of his pots. The decoration of the ware can be precisely planned—incised, poured over wax or silk-screened—but the final change is wrought by the kiln, the melting, vitrifying, the emergence of the colour, and sometimes the permanent sticking to the kiln shelf. It is no wonder that a potter sometimes credits his kiln with a kind of creative intelligence which he tries to master or placate.

Every potter who has fired his own work, rather than handed it over to a technician to nurse, knows the special experience of opening up or unbricking the door of a cooling kiln, and seeing his finished work for the first time in the pinging, quivering atmosphere of a fresh firing. So often the pots seem small and unimportant, the colours too dull, too bright, or the surfaces too dry. Bryan Newman, who made the large coil pot illustrated opposite, expresses it vividly:

I sometimes wonder why I ever took up pottery when I open the kiln door and everything that comes out is so insignificant compared to what I had imagined ... but by some sort of recuperative magic, a few days later I'm back at it again ... and dreaming how marvellous everything will look.

And sometimes it does. The 'cookery' of glaze recipes means the infinite permutations of a handful of ingredients, and one day experiments will throw up a really wonderful texture, a perfect combination of colour and surface to compliment a perfect shape. Hans Coper, limiting himself to a well-tried combination of clay and glaze, strives like a musician practising to achieve an ever purer result. Why all this striving? It is like asking why a bird keeps on singing, or why a man climbs up a mountain. And if the potter's work has the spirited joy of a bird's song, he shares the aches and pains of a mountaineer.

It is the arms and the back which suffer most. He may find himself 'wedging', or preparing, ten hundredweights of clay in a morning, and this leaves little strength for throwing pots on the wheel in the afternoon, still less for the stern aesthetic appraisal of his own work which he cannot afford to ignore.

A visit to a studio pottery is an exciting experience, even for the most uninvolved amateur. By the very nature of the ceramic process, because of the time dependence of the potter working

with a material which cannot be hurried, there is always something to see in every stage of the making. Bags of powdered clay lie around as in a flour mill, and there is often an old baker's dough mixer requisitioned to make a smooth clay 'body'. The raw materials lie side by side with dark grey leathery pots, made some hours before, which are drying, plaster moulds for making bowls and saucers, and white 'once-fired' porous pots waiting to be glazed. There are cool, deliberately damp cupboards, and the hot, dry kiln room. Often on the walls there are pottery shapes, drawn with a clayey finger, for reference. There is usually a kettle, too, but like a watchmaker who can never tell you the time, the potter rarely knows where he can put his hand on a cup or mug for making tea.

The potter is a truly romantic figure, at once at grips with nature and with the modern world. His materials are commonplace, ubiquitous, too, which is fortunate because they are so heavy and expensive to transport. His artistic heritage is frightening; unlike the sculptor, he is dogged by the uneasy feeling that what he is doing ought to be functional, and by the certain knowledge that a modern factory can always produce an article

Making a Pot 236

which will function better than his own. He is naggingly aware that there is a market for his work not because it is good but because it is 'rustic', handmade, an anachronism. He yearns as an artist to make a relevant contribution to the art of his time.

It is nearly fifty years since Bernard Leach set up, in the dark days of hand-made pottery in Britain, his now famous studio at St Ives, and set welcome standards of purity and simplicity in design. But the oriental inspiration which guided his work now seems not only irrelevant but a positive hindrance to vitality and expression in the present day. Potters in America and in Western Europe are asserting that their medium is as appropriate as stone or metal for three-dimensional design and bas-relief, and they are challenging the assumption that pottery must be hollow, that a pot must be a useful container. Particularly in America, ceramic sculpture is being made on the same scale as sculpture in bronze, for there is virtually no limit to the size or weight of a pot which can be fired by modern techniques. It is indeed a wonderful experience to see a material which has been too long in an abstract or utilitarian limbo suddenly flowering with expressive force, and coming to the frontier of the fine arts. But pottery does not need to be big to be modern; nor does it need to be trivial if it is small, and a pot certainly seems more satisfying if it is scaled to the human hand, and can be picked up, or at least lifted, rather than walked around.

Every collector knows the delight of owning and holding a wonderful pot; not because it serves a function, or represents something, or even because it reflects an era or because it is old, but simply because it looks and feels beautiful. And it is all the more exciting if you have had a hand in the making.

The exciting shapes of minarets around Turkish mosques made the author experiment with a series of tower pots, piling wheel-made or 'thrown' units on the top of tall slender bases. As the series progressed, bulbous forms were used to crown the stems. These stems were thrown first, and allowed to dry so that they would be strong enough to support the wide tops. All the pots shown opposite are made from coarse open-structured clay, and are glazed inside to make them watertight. Using a broad brush, the outsides are coated with a liquid mixture of wood ash and clay, which burns to a honey-gold at a temperature of 1280°C. The small vase in the foreground is made in one piece, and glazed inside with flinty blue.

Every part of each pot shown on these two pages has been made on the wheel, assembled and modified as the clay passes from a wet state into the stage potters know as 'leather hard'. For some twenty years Hans Coper has been making pots with similar shapes and parts, although he never makes two pots which are alike. The bi-symmetrical form, right, is made in two pieces, stem and bowl, with the bowl scored on both sides as the clay dries, so that it looks organic, like a dividing cell. Manganese oxide, which is dark chocolate brown, covers the inside of the pot and, rubbed into the rough surface on the outside, emphasises the texture of the pot like suture lines on a bone.

The large pot on the left stands nearly 18 in. high. The great bell-like base was made on the wheel in one piece, and finished to mathematical precision with a metal tool. The top, also wheel-thrown in one piece, was squeezed, cut to shape and slipped over the base, the intersections smoothed with soft clay. The top, made oval by the squeezing, became gently undulating as the shape it terminates was pulled apart to straddle the base. Again, dark brown manganese oxide covers the inside, but is carefully wiped off the white rim.

In the smaller pot on the right, one cylinder, nearly flattened out, is thrust into the jaws of another. The spade shape at the top is precisely pre-determined by the form made on the wheel: in this instance it was rather like a plant pot before it was flattened. The clay is white, and the scored surface is covered with a thin coat of liquid clay, called 'slip', which makes the pot look ghostly, apparently translucent.

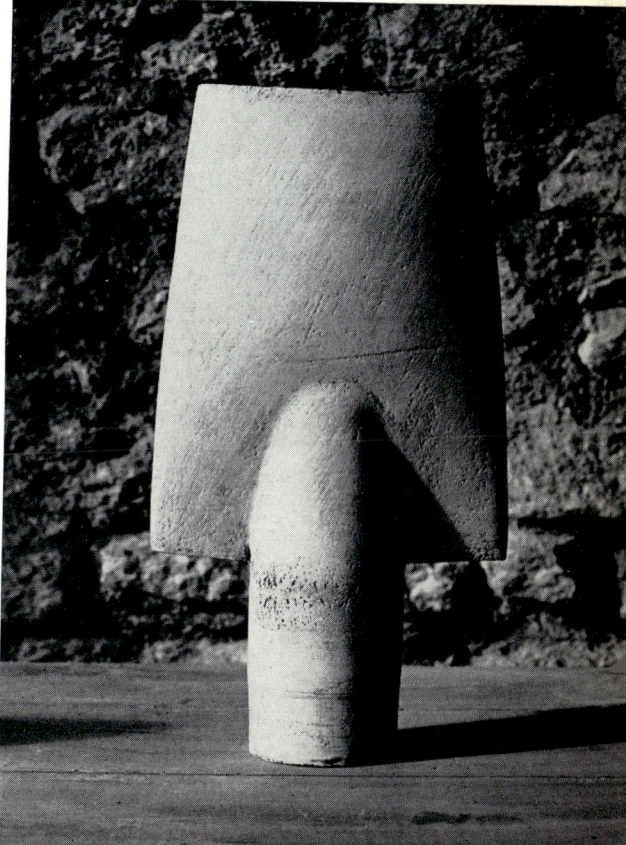

Bryan Newman, unlike many contemporary potters, is not troubled by questions of definition and validity when his work approaches sculpture. He simply makes what he wants to make, quickly, deftly, and with humour. Like a hairdresser, he adapts his material with a fine sense of improvisation. The teapot fantasies shown on these pages may contain up to fifty individually thrown items, assembled as the superstructure to a barrel-shaped body. The little teapot, lower left, actually works: it is glazed inside, and covered outside with a dry indian red clay 'slip'.

The more complex construction, top left, abandons all function. Its barrel is made in two pieces, joined at the middle, and the screen construction above is formed by cutting sections from wheel-thrown shallow cylinders and sticking them together with water when the clay is just hard enough to bear its own weight, but still soft enough to be bent into shape without losing its 'spring'. The surface coating contains copper and cobalt, and the colour is dark blue-green.

The construction above, looking like a disconsolate traction engine, has details in its superstructure squared off with a sharp knife. Painted with cobalt and iron, it is dark blue and ochre coloured, and stands precariously on one leg.

A twelve-inch hollow cube of clay makes an excellent seat, although it is rather cold. It certainly was not designed by Anthony Hepburn to have any function at all. Fascinated by the technique of 'slab building', and in particular by the wobbly failures made by students trying to build large slab-sided pots out of clay, he deliberately set out to capture the moment of crumpling, bending and collapsing. The result was a celebrated series of pots in which hard, fired clay looked rubbery, and clumps of skittle-like forms, vitrified together in the kiln, captured and froze the dynamic moment of impact in a skittle alley. Influenced by American painters like Warhol who take as study material the expendable packaging of mass products, Hepburn has gift-wrapped his clay box with brilliant purple stripes, using masking tape to keep the edges crisp.

It is difficult to think of bricks as anything other than hard, rectilinear units. When Anthony Hepburn worked in a brick factory he was fascinated to see soft wet bricks, fresh from the mould, occasionally slip to the floor. Carefully retrieving the misshapen blocks, he fired them at home in his own kiln. He went on to make a mould of a brick, from which he could cast hollow units, and build the 'plinthoi' for his ceramic constructions. One exciting result, shown above, is a crushed hollow brick, draped with coarse cloth. For centuries the crinolines of porcelain figures have been made by soaking fabric in wet clay, and letting the fibres burn away in the kiln to leave a hard filigree of ceramic lace. When the technique is applied to coarse cloth, known as 'sculptor's scrim', a most unusual texture is the result. The spiky, skeletal structure transmuted from the cloth makes a strong counterpoint to the limp shape of the brick. The glaze is cream-coloured.

It is very difficult to manage without an eggcup. A boiled egg is usually too hot to hold, and it must be gripped by something which is the right shape and the right size. This group of eggcups by Melchior Wyt shows how exciting an everyday pot can be when the designer takes a fresh look at the forms best suited to the job. Wyt's eggcups are heavy enough not to fall over, and they are not glazed on the base so that they cannot slide about on a plate. Cast from plaster moulds, they are glazed in white.

VESTA TILLEY

Male Impersonators
BY DAVID CHESHIRE

'THERE SHE WAS, the complete man of the world, in perfectly cut clothes of the most fashionable kind, with everything correct, down to the collar studs and cufflinks, for she gave infinite attention to detail; whether she appeared as a policeman, a sailor, a soldier or what you will, there was no flaw of any kind. In one of her songs she smoked a cigar as to the manner born, yet with it all, she was always a woman with a woman's charm and fascination, whatever her outward appearance she never lost femininity.'

W. Macqueen Pope's description of Vesta Tilley must sum up also the general effect achieved by all the other women who have presented themselves variously in man's guise on stage and screen. And perversely enough, no sooner had women won the right to appear on public stages at all—following the Restoration of Charles II—than they started to impersonate men, and not only in those parts written for the Elizabethan boy-actors. The latter had found themselves frequently, of course, rather ambiguously dressing themselves up as women dressing up as men. When actresses arrived they immediately monopolised these roles, and only in boys' school productions (and the recent National Theatre *As You Like It*) have the plays been seen as Shakespeare envisaged them. The female impersonation seems to be an integral part of the plot, especially in the comedies, where the enigmatic, androgynous character so produced is one of the many nuances of a Shakespearean plot obliterated when an actress is involved.

Nevertheless virtually every major actress (of either comedy or tragedy) has scored at least one of her biggest successes in a Shakespearean role—sometimes even in a genuine male role. Hamlet—the most obviously 'feminine' of the major tragic heroes—is usually the chosen one, but there is the curious case of Priscilla Horton who played the Fool in William Macready's 1838 revival of the true 'unadapted' text of *King Lear*. Macready had imagined the Fool as 'a fragile, hectic, beautiful-faced, half-idiot-looking boy'. A colleague suggested immediately that 'a woman should play it'. Miss Horton also played Ariel, but other actresses have appeared in that part.

Sarah Siddons was reputedly the first female Hamlet, and Siobhan McKenna's appearance in the role in New York in 1957 was one of the most recent. But undoubtedly the most famous female Hamlet was Sarah Bernhardt's. She spoke a French translation, of course, but Clement Scott maintained she was exquisite, and that only she among all her contemporaries caught Hamlet's essential 'eccentric capriciousness'. Max Beerbohm, however, declared: 'I cannot imagine anyone . . . taking it seriously,' adding that the polite British audience typically restrained its laughter until it was outside the theatre.

The Divine Sarah *chose* to play Hamlet (and a dozen other male roles) and the first great American actress—Charlotte Cushman —*chose* to play Macbeth, Wolsey, and Romeo, with enormous critical acclaim, as an intellectual challenge; but some actresses have had male costume thrust on them in the exigencies of the service. Thus Sybil Thorndike played Prince Hal, Ferdinand, Launcelot Gobbo, and Chorus, as well as Katharine, in *Henry V*, at the Old Vic during the First Great War. Actresses still appear as schoolboys in some provincial repertory companies when the occasion demands; but there again economics, not a desire for a show-business 'gimmick', make such impersonations necessary.

During the Restoration and the eighteenth century, however, it was purely the need for a sensational eye-catcher that caused so many dramatists to provide rôles for so many actresses to display themselves in men's apparel. These 'breeches parts', as they were called, became so popular that managers dressed actresses as men on the slightest pretext, until even such an ardent admirer of the female form as Samuel Pepys began to tire of the fad. The enormous popularity of the eighteenth-century's best comic actresses—Peg Woffington, Anne Barry and Dorothy Jordan— depended a great deal upon their many successful breeches parts. Peg Woffington (who at one point in her notoriously promiscuous career set up a *ménage à trois* with both the foremost actors of her day—Charles Macklin and David Garrick) scored big hits as Lothario and Captain Macheath. So sure was

Anne Barry as Sir Harry Wildair in Farquhar's *The Constant Couple*, 1771

she of her powers as a male impersonator that after a performance as Sir Harry Wildair in Farquhar's *The Constant Couple* she boasted to the Green Room that she believed half the audience had taken her for a real man. A colleague quickly pointed out that the other half could readily convince them to the contrary. The private life of Mrs. Jordan (by whom the Duke of Clarence—later William IV—had ten illegitimate children) would also seem to prove convincingly that it was most definitely not lesbian tendencies that caused so many personable young ladies to don male attire so frequently.

Although psychologists might say that the pioneer actresses (Nell Gwyn among them) were keen to play male rôles to show that they were the equal of any actor, the real reason was almost certainly not quite so intellectual. The dictates of seventeenth- and eighteenth-century fashion meant that no matter how *décolleté* a dress might be, to show an ankle would be extremely immodest. What more obvious way for a suitably endowed actress to show that she had legs than to appear as a man?

Of the scores of breeches parts created to meet public demand virtually only Silvia in Farquhar's *The Recruiting Officer* and Beatrice in Goldoni's *Servant of Two Masters* have survived into the modern repertoire—outside opera houses. In opera true breeches parts are still regularly seen. Kathleen Ferrier's most famous rôle—*Orfeo*—was written originally for a castrato singer, but Leonora in Beethoven's *Fidelio,* Hansel in Humperdinck's *Hansel and Gretel,* Cherubino in Mozart's *Marriage of Figaro,* and Octavian in Strauss' *Der Rosenkavalier* (written at the height of the British male impersonator boom in 1910) are all scored for and sung by women.

As Brecht's *The Good Woman of Setzuan*, in which 'The Good Woman' (a prostitute) has frequently to transform herself into her bestial male cousin, is not often seen in Britain, the only play regularly presented which demands an actress in a male rôle is Barrie's *Peter Pan*. But even though many eminent actresses—usually nowadays from film or television—have appeared in its annual revival the heavily cut version presented today would not seem to allow the Peter to catch the true magic of the part as Barrie wrote it, and in which Nina Boucicault, Jean Forbes-Robertson and Pauline Chase, for example, achieved great popularity. Gradually, Peter has become merely another Principal Boy, in which type of rôle also the more successful practitioners must try to suppress their sex appeal, and make 'no pretence at masculine arrogance, no suggestion of feminine wile'.

It must be admitted, however, that one of the essential assets of an acceptable Principal Boy is 'a good pair of legs'. Presumably it was always so, and prints of the earliest Principal Boys (and indeed the breeches-part players) confirm this opinion. The two types of part are closely linked, for it was as the breeches part declined in public favour that the Extravaganza began to be a dominant form on the British theatrical scene. Madame Vestris gave the Extravaganza an enormous boost when she dazzled London with her own productions at the Olympic Theatre in the 1830s, with herself in the leading rôles—most notably in Planché's punning adaptations of Perrault's fairy tales, the direct ancestors of the modern pantomime. Today the female Principal Boy is not seen as frequently as she might be. Men are cast as the heroes, allegedly because the public demands realism (even in pantomime?); but possibly the real reason is that there are just not enough actresses (for obviously they have to be able to act as well as sing) with enough stage-presence to carry off the part with any conviction, and stage-presence is one of the elements frequently lacking in the young 'pop' singers who should be playing these roles.

By all accounts stage presence was distinctly *not* lacking in the performances of those women who presented themselves as male impersonators and nothing more during what is often reputed to be the Golden Age of the Music Hall—the thirty years preceding 1914.

An early photograph of Vesta Tilley shows her dressed for her solo turn in what is virtually the current Principal Boy's outfit; but she soon changed into correct fashionable men's clothes for the still-heard character songs ('After the Ball', 'Burlington Bertie', etc.) in which she satirised good-naturedly the behaviour of the contemporary young men about town, and in which indeed (according to R. J. Minney in *The Edwardian Age*) she set the fashion for many, especially those returning from service in the Colonies. They would arrange to meet old friends at the Empire, Leicester Square, and glance 'only occasionally at the stage to learn from Vesta Tilley . . . turned out by Savile Row, what the best-dressed man should be wearing'. Her success led many others to become male impersonators, including Ella Shields who was still asking someone to 'Show me the way to go home' in the 1940s, and Hetty King who was still insisting that 'All the nice girls love a sailor' even in the 1960s.

But both were exceptions, and the male impersonator's popularity was beginning to fade even before Vesta Tilley made her farewell appearance at the Coliseum in 1920. It cannot really be entirely coincidental that her career spanned the years of the Feminist Revolt, when women were trying to play an active part in the political life of the country, and pursue careers in their chosen professions, just as easily as actresses had since 1660. The Great War, perhaps even more than the efforts of the Suffragettes, had hastened female emancipation, just as much as it had familiarised the idea of women in men's clothing (perhaps slightly modified) in the streets. Many women chose to wear these mannish clothes not because they were lesbians, but because the non-working-class woman wanted a simpler and more convenient mode of dress in which to undertake everyday jobs as readily as men, jobs not possible in the elaborate coiffures and dresses High Fashion decreed. As Simone de Beauvoir stressed in *The Second Sex*: 'The heterosexual feminists . . . declining to make themselves merchandise . . . affected severe tailor-made suits . . . elaborate low-necked gowns seemed to them symbolical of the social order they were fighting.' Similar dress was (and is) adopted by many lesbians, and this is why that subject is as frequently raised in discussions on male impersonation as homosexuality is in those on female impersonation.

Roger Baker very clearly explains the essential difference between the two forms of theatrical transvestism in his book on *Drag* (significantly enough there is no similar word to describe male impersonation): 'male impersonation is . . . a far more devious manifestation with a more complex sexual and social significance ... it is used with more freedom, is better documented and would appear to have older and deeper traditions of social approval ... When a woman disguises herself as a man she is accentuating her own sex appeal, whereas a man dressing up as a woman debases or annihilates his own sexual character ... Women dressed up as men do not produce the same set of responses as a female impersonator,' which is presumably why even though there is far more male impersonation on the amateur stage today than there is female impersonation, it is the latter that receives the most publicity.

Simone de Beauvoir also suggested that some women adopt mannish clothes because they are more becoming. This was certainly the case with Marlene Dietrich, who gave the tradition of male impersonation a lengthy run in cabaret and the cinema, even after its popularity in the theatre had declined. It may be that Dietrich appeared in male dress to prove that her sensual appeal did not depend entirely upon her legendary legs. But with Dietrich (as with Greta Garbo) the donning of a man's uniform becomes slightly equivocal. Josef von Sternberg, director of Dietrich's first Hollywood film—*Morocco*—was undoubtedly aware of this aspect of her allure, and, in his book on Sternberg, Andrew Sarris vividly describes the impact on the audience 'when Dietrich materialises in top hat, white tie, and tails'. She is 'thereafter immortalised as the purveyor of pan-sexuality . . . Aside from the lilting vertiginousness of vice involved in Marlene's mock seduction of a flustered female, Sternberg achieves all sorts of economies of expression in Marlene's masterful masquerade. Her costume, for example, mocks [Adolphe] Menjou's. Here is a representation of the civilised European male as seen from the point of view of the woman he seeks to seduce ... but yet the effect is not one of pure parody ... there is always chance, romance, and the inspiration of improvisation. Dietrich fondles the hair of the girl she is going to outrage with a kiss, but she has none of the complacent confidence Garbo displays in a similar situation in *Queen Christina*. Dietrich's impersonation is an adventure, an act of bravado. . . .' Whereas when Garbo played Queen Christina (interestingly enough her favourite rôle) she was able in a true 'breeches part'

Male Impersonators 252

scene—the Queen travelling disguised as a man is forced to share a bedroom with the Spanish Ambassador, and so reveal her true sex—'to convert', in Alexander Walker's phrase, 'her enigmatic sexual status into very real power'.

Usually, however, male impersonation has been used in films either as a joke or as a dance-routine feature. The 1935 adaptation of Compton Mackenzie's *Sylvia Scarlett*, however, enabled Katharine Hepburn to give a fascinating performance in boy's clothes in a picaresque tale which allows plenty of opportunities for almost Shakespearean scenes of mistaken sexual identity. François Truffaut's *Jules et Jim* contained one sequence in which Jeanne Moreau dressed up (according to the screenplay) as Charlie Chaplin's *The Kid*. The result looks nothing like Jackie Coogan, but the narrator makes the following comment after the scene is over: 'Catherine was very pleased with the success of her disguise. Jules and Jim were moved, as if by a symbol which they did not understand.' Possibly similar reactions have greeted male impersonators since they first appeared on the scene.

Although the Queen appears often on public occasions in feminised male uniforms, Her Majesty's performances as a pantomime Principal Boy have been held in private at Windsor Castle. The photograph opposite shows the 1941 production of *Cinderella*, with Princess Margaret in the name part (Radio Times Hulton Picture Library).

With the exception of this photograph, and the stills from the British Film Archive which follow, the illustrations to this feature are from the Mander and Mitchenson Theatre Collection.

Above: Marlene Dietrich in Josef von Sternberg's *Morocco* (Paramount), 1930.

At the top of the page opposite are Hetty King in a characteristic music-hall act, and Sarah Bernhardt as Hamlet. Below are Greta Garbo in Rouben Mamoulian's *Queen Christina* (M.G.M.), 1933, and Katharine Hepburn in George Cukor's *Sylvia Scarlett* (R.K.O.), 1935.

On the right is Jeanne Moreau, supposedly dressed as Jackie Coogan in *The Kid*, as she appeared in François Truffaut's *Jules et Jim*, 1961 (Gala Films).

The original Peter Pan, Nina Boucicault in the first production, 1904, at the Duke of York's Theatre, London.

3/70

WITHDRAWN

Minneapolis Public Library

1970

The borrower is responsible for all materials drawn on his card and for fines on overdue items. Marking and mutilation of books are prohibited, and are punishable by law.